CAMP

STORIES & ITINERARIES
for SLEEPING UNDER THE STARS

CAMP

LUC GESELL

with **NICHOLAS LOVECCHIO**

CLARKSON POTTER/PUBLISHERS
NEW YORK

TO ALL MY
OUTDOOR-LOVING FRIENDS.

And to Fanny, partner in
my greatest life adventures—
at camp, at home, and between.

Pond in the Berkshires, Massachusetts
Contributed by Kyle Finn Dempsey

CONTENTS

INTRODUCTION

IMAGINE WAKING UP at the beginning of a cold morning and unzipping your tent to take in an endless horizon. Your body feels a bit stiff from sleeping on the ground, but your ears perk up to new sounds you haven't heard in a while–perhaps chattering birds or a trickling stream. You step out to your campsite, which might be tucked in a national park, perched on the edge of a cliff, or set up on a beach just out of reach of the tides. You're far away from your familiar surroundings–along with all of the stress that comes with it. You smile to yourself and set to work brewing coffee and cooking breakfast in what has always been humankind's first home: Nature.

From Alastair Humphreys's notion of microadventures (page 12) to Grace McDonald's extreme basecamping in the Himalayas (pages 197–99), this book covers an inexhaustible amount of inspiration and outdoor opportunities to seize upon. You might like camping with a dog, like Abigail LaFleur-Shaffer and Kuma (pages 28–35), as a family like Sarah Whiteman and her kids (page 54), or by yourself on a bucket-list thru-hike (pages 78–79)–whatever your #camplife, my hope is that you'll find new ideas to try out on your next adventure.

Because everyone has a different way of going about it–as well as different motivations–I've found that camping can't be expressed only through a list of required gear or a manual of best practices. Equipment and techniques are important, but they are not enough to define it. The best outdoor adventures begin with some inspiration, usually through stories about others' travels. And in this book, you'll hear from dozens of explorers, enjoy hundreds of their impressive photographs of faraway places, and learn essential tips for setting up your tent, building a fire, cooking a meal, and more. Even if you're a complete novice, you might find yourself living vicariously through, say, a photo of a tent suspended ten thousand feet up. No doubt you'll sense the dizzying height, the risk and effort, the inaccessibility of the campsite–but then I bet many of you will experience the desire to seek out that spot, along with the curiosity, the dream, and the *Why not me?*

However you choose to camp, what's important is that you do it. As they say, there's no time like the present, when we're all living in a world that's changing entirely too quickly. Life outdoors is an extraordinary opportunity to reconnect with our earth at a time when it is more urgent and meaningful than ever.

Enjoying my morning coffee in the
French Pyrénées Mountains
Contributed by Matthieu Tober

"Thousands of tired,
nerve-shaken,
over-civilized people
are beginning to
find out that going
to the mountains
is going home;
that wilderness is
a necessity."

—JOHN MUIR

Hipcamp spot in the valley of
Yosemite National Park
Contributed by Clara Aranovich

THE
ESCAPE

A GREAT CAMPING TRIP CAN BE AS SIMPLE as seeking nearby grounds where you can pitch a shelter, however grand or modest. You don't have to venture too far, nor do you have to brave uncomfortable, cold, or damp conditions. If you're missing a sleeping bag, you can still experience the thrill of nature while tucked into the warmth of a wool blanket. The simple act of sleeping outside is already an experience in its own right—a "microadventure," to use the English adventurer Alastair Humphreys's phrase, where the idea of getting away from it all is easily achieved. And if you're new to camping, your first night outside might be in your backyard; your second, perhaps on the outskirts of town. You'll be hard-pressed to find a city or town in the world without some forest, field, or garden ready to welcome you.

PREVIOUS AND ABOVE The art of setting up camp

Contributed by Matt Miller

THE COMFORT
OF CAMPING

When you camp, you may wish to seek out little luxuries and
reminders of home in nature. You pack tokens—items from your
home to help put you at ease while you're away—into a backpack,
or a car trunk, and head off to live outside for a short while.
Taking the dog for a walk, reading by the fireplace, cooking
dinner—you can transpose these everyday activities to the great
outdoors for greater enjoyment in the wilderness. Your dog may
not be running in the park but in the woods, your stove will be a
campfire, and you'll get to dine under the stars . . .

This chapter is about easy access to the wildlife and the
not-so-secret doors that lead to memorable camping trips. Allow
these stories, tips, and testimonies to inspire and encourage you
to take a little break from your ever more hectic days. It may
prove challenging to get started, but you'll return refreshed and
at peace after living the slow life.

"Nothing beats
waking up
with fresh air
in your lungs
on a cold
morning."

THE OUTDOOR MINDSET

with Mason Strehl

MASON STREHL is a Washington State–based outdoor photographer. For him, the true appeal of camping is being with friends. Mason tells us more about how he approaches outdoor life: by keeping one leg in his home life and the other in his camp life, he can jump from one to the other very easily. He constantly seeks out inspiration for new spots to explore, and he's always refreshing the weather forecast website.

How often do you camp? And what has been your favorite experience?

I go camping about twice a month. Life can get very busy, but it's important to step back and take time to reset in nature. I prefer to go during the week or over the holidays, as it's always less crowded. Summertime is especially great for hanging outside, but lately I've been getting very interested in winter camping.

What do you expect from camping?

Nature is where I'm happiest—nothing beats waking up with fresh air in your lungs on a cold morning. So in the process of trying to spend every minute I can outdoors, it makes sense I would sleep out there when possible. I am a strong believer that people get too comfortable in their everyday life; camping provides an escape from comfort and makes you feel alive.

Do you camp with friends?

I often camp alone, but being outdoors with friends and like-minded people is an amazing and irreplaceable feeling. I also love teaching people about the outdoors: how to find the best sites, build fires, pitch tents, and everything that comes with camping. All of it is an art, and not many people know how to do it.

How far do you go?

I usually camp fairly close to home—within a three-hour drive. I do this because often my camp trips are impulsive. I keep all my camp gear packed and may decide to go camping only an hour or two before I leave.

What do you need to make a camp trip great?

There are three things that make camp trips great: campfires, friends, and beer. If you have at least two of those things you'll have an amazing time, but all three is heaven.

OPPOSITE TOP Self-portrait

OPPOSITE At Slaughter Ridge, on the heights of Kenai Lake, Alaska
Contributed by Mason Strehl

MASON'S ESSENTIALS
FOR A WEEKEND TRIP

- Axe
- Sierra Designs Clip Flashlight Tent
- Zenbivy sleeping bag
- Thermarest Prolite Sleeping Pad
- Canon 5D Mark III camera

SWEDEN: THE CAPITAL OF CAMPING

Many countries could vie for the title of Camping Capital of the World for their legendary trails, their breathtaking scenery, or the diversity of their wilderness. The United States, Canada, Argentina, or Germany—to name just a few—would be good contenders. But there's one country on the Arctic's doorstep where, beyond all those wonders, another defining feature rules: the freedom to roam.

Much of Swedish culture is based on the right of common access to nature—one that's legally enshrined in Sweden's constitution. Anyone can decide to pitch a tent in the country's vast open spaces. Maybe you're still thinking your country can hold its own. But Swedish law goes even further, allowing you to venture onto private land and spend a night there without the owner's permission.

But with all rights come responsibilities. In this case, it's your responsibility to preserve and protect nature, to leave the land you traverse as untouched as it was when you arrived. For the Swedes, the wilderness is their home, so they naturally want to take care of its flora and fauna, water, rocks, and minerals.

The freedom to roam, or *allemansrätten*, applies to all visitors, not just to Swedish citizens. If you're traveling in Sweden, don't miss out on the opportunity to spend a night in the great outdoors (and make sure you understand the responsibilities that come with it by visiting Sweden's tourism website). Nature can be found everywhere in this beautiful country—from its wildest, most remote corners to its biggest metropolises. If you have more time, try hiking the Kungsleden (King's Trail) or near Trollsjön (Troll Lake, also called Rissajaure) (see page 175).

Troll Lake in Kärkevagge Valley, northern Sweden
Contributed by Lisa Löwenborg

CAMPING
CHRONICLES

Mason Strehl

SLEEPING IN A CLOUD AT
MOUNT BAKER. WASHINGTON STATE

The wind felt good as it streamed in the open window. The mountains grew as we sped toward Mount Baker. We figured we'd hike in, find a nice spot by a lake, and camp for the night before heading home.

As we arrived at the trailhead, clouds began to roll in. We were a little disappointed at the change in weather, but we headed out on the trail undeterred. We hiked for several hours, stopping by lakes and overlooks, snacking all along the way. During one of these stops, I took off on a solo adventure to see if I could find a good campsite for the night. I hiked about two miles uphill and off the trail to a little nook I saw tucked away. It was the perfect spot, with a firepit already built. I quickly ran back and told the rest of the group. Everyone gathered their gear, and we hiked to the spot where we would spend the night.

Just as we finished setting up camp, the clouds cleared away, revealing an incredible view of Mount Baker. We sat around our fire, sharing stories and taking in the sheer beauty of the scene as the sun set. Slowly the stars came out, and slowly everyone retired to their tents.

I slept soundly through the night, and when I woke up, I poked my head out of the tent. I could barely see 20 feet in front of me because of the thick fog that had encroached on our camp. It made for a beautiful scene and isolated us from the rest of the world. It was hard to pack up and go home.

Along Chain Lakes Trail, a few kilometers
from Artist Point, Washington State
Contributed by Mason Strehl

HOW TO FIND A CAMPSITE

with Alyssa Ravasio

In the United States, where approximately 60 percent of the land is privately owned, **ALYSSA RAVASIO**, founder of the California-based startup Hipcamp, is unleashing the power of private land so that anyone, wherever they live, can find a spot to pitch a tent and reconnect with nature. This is the mission of Hipcamp, which grew out of the frustration Alyssa felt one day as she watched "gorgeous, glassy, barreling waves" crashing against the Big Sur coast at Andrew Molera State Park. "When I actually arrived at the campground," she said, "I found out that even though I'd read so much about this place, I had not learned that it was home to a great surf break." Feeling forlorn, Alyssa watched as amazing waves broke along the shore without her—for this surf bum had left her board at home.

Finding a good place to camp—and knowing what to expect when you get there—shouldn't be so complicated. After all, we have access to excellent local reviews of restaurants and hotels before we book a trip—why shouldn't we have access to the same level of information about campsites? So she poured all her energy into connecting potential campers to landowners and locals who know the land.

What exactly are the kinds of grounds we can camp on using Hipcamp?

People can find anything from nature preserves to ranches to farms—a huge range, really. If it's a place where people are going to explore nature, it can be on Hipcamp. Anyone can get involved who takes good care of their land and who is interested in sharing it with other nature lovers (and earning some income, too!).

What are some of the day-to-day results of increased camping?

I think when people spend time in nature, they become better versions of themselves. They remember what matters. New science shows us people become less stressed, more creative, and more grateful with time in nature. It's also the key to developing a reciprocal relationship with the rest of the natural world: When nature is giving so much to you, you can't help but want to help take care of it.

Camping is sometimes hard on nature.

You have to be smart about minimizing your impact on nature. Especially in popular areas, it's important to follow marked trails and the like. But it's so important to get people outside and caring about nature. People protect what they love.

A Hipcamp spot with a view of Half Dome in Yosemite National Park, California
Contributed by Sarah Vaughn

How will Hipcamp affect crowded national park campsites?
We are definitely interested in spreading out and redistributing use. It's better for people and the environment. Although sometimes people stay at a Hipcamp so that they can also visit a national park like Yosemite or Yellowstone.

Do you have a message for campers?
Nature is our home! By spending time outside, you can improve your mental, physical, and spiritual well-being. And by staying on Hipcamps, you can learn all about how people are taking care of their land, and in turn, you'll see a future for humanity where people are part of nature—living with it in harmony.

"Spending time outdoors has proven health benefits and fosters a deeper connection to the awesome, wild world out there."

GET AWAY
BY GOING HOME

A great escape can be had anywhere outdoors where you feel good vibes and where you can set down a piece of home, think, and be open to new perspectives. A favorite campsite can present infinite possibilities and does not need to be located far from where you live.

Kyle Finn Dempsey spent his childhood in the Berkshires with a kind of detachment, simply enjoying it, but with an eye on the world outside and the will to explore it. When he became an adult, though, he realized how far one can get by staying nearby–especially when you're lucky enough to call such a beautiful place home.

Only a ten-minute drive from his house, Kyle's favorite spot is the same place he grew up spending his summers. He calls it Salamander Cove, because he and his childhood friends always used to catch lizards there, in the weeds around the edges. This paradise "has a nice little beach and an island on the far end. All around the edges are little coves in the rhododendron bushes, with pine needle floors and rocky landings."

In the summer of 2016, Kyle had just quit his job and was spending his days at the pond, trying to figure out what path he wanted to head down–photography, music, marketing? It was at that moment when he realized the Berkshires were a whole world to explore, with hundreds of camp spots hidden on

"No need to travel the world to find great camp spots for unique and unforgettable moments."

islands or perched along the banks. Salamander Cove became a place of refuge and therapy for him, the spot he decided to return to for the rest of his life.

Nestled in the western third of Massachusetts and Connecticut, the Berkshires are an ancient range of rolling hills filled with quaint little towns, rivers and ponds, and dirt roads lined with old stone walls. "The people here are deeply connected with the land and spend much of their time outside camping, fishing, hunting, and exploring," says Kyle. This is his camping territory. He grew up pitching tents near these ponds as often as possible, and, now in his twenties, he still does. With his camping essentials, fishing gear, and some musical instruments in tow, he travels by canoe "around the edges and on the islands, freeing my mind from all the modern-day stress."

As a social media influencer who shares his adventures with his followers, Kyle has become a great ambassador of his homeland—a "Berkshires storyteller." Find inspiration on Kyle's Instagram gallery (@kylefinndempsey) and learn how to make your homeland your own campground. And maybe it'll become a life project.

PREVIOUS AND OPPOSITE
Ponds in the Berkshires, MA
Contributed by Kyle Finn Dempsey

DOG CAMPING

If you're like Abigail LaFleur-Shaffer, you love hiking as much as you love your dog. So why not turn your weekend dog-walking sessions into an accessible adventure of hiking and sleeping outdoors together? Just check that the campsite and trails allow dogs. Abigail and her Siberian husky, Kuma, have started doing just this in their backyard of Colorado, a gold mine for humans and their pets.

The idea of bringing your dog into the wild might sound insurmountable when you consider the organization, care, and accessibility aspects, not to mention the other wildlife you might encounter. I thought that, too, but in talking with Abigail, I realized that there's something very instinctive about camping out with a dog.

"Packing for a trip with my dog is definitely different from packing for a trip without my dog," Abigail explains. But she also points out, "It's not much more work." You need to keep the same things in mind for your dog as for you: food, safety, rules, and well-being. If you're feeling tired, hungry, thirsty, or in danger, your dog probably feels the same. Abigail always tries to pack as light as she can, even for the two of them. "I simply have to pack enough food–and some extra just in case we get lost, stranded, or decide to stay an extra day or two–and his essentials."

The good news is your dog, just like you, has a back and shoulders. Abigail doesn't hesitate to deck Kuma out with a backpack. Indeed, she knows her dog is quite capable of hauling his own gear. Plus, it lightens the load on her own back, letting her pick up the hiking pace when needed (especially in the case of rain). Of course, you don't have to saddle your dog up with gear if you don't feel comfortable doing so. And before he begins

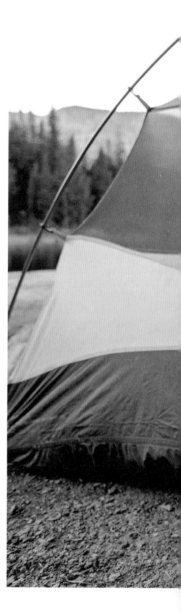

"There's something very instinctive about camping with a dog."

Dog camping in Northern Colorado
Contributed by Abigail LaFleur-Shaffer

DOG PACK ESSENTIALS

- Biodegradable pet waste bags
- First aid kit
- Leash and/or off-leash collar
- Water filter or purifier
- Water bowl
- Blanket
- Sleeping pad
- Lightweight food
- Lots of treats!

carrying a pack, you want to make sure his bones have fully developed. Don't try this with puppies.

Before you focus on what is inside the pack, you first need to think about the pack itself. Start by measuring the broadest part of your dog's rib cage. Use that girth measurement when shopping for the right size. Beyond the diameter of your dog's chest, the size of your dog will also determine the capacity of load of the pack.

Then, take it for a test walk before you load it up. Indeed, during your first training walk, you want to fit your dog with an empty pack. Little by little, load the pack with his stuff, with the weight on each side equally distributed, and see how he reacts. Watch your dog's breath. As long as he's not breathless, then you can add more essentials.

PREVIOUS Hiking the dog-friendly trails in
Winter Park, Colorado, and Oregon
Contributed by Abigail LaFleur-Shaffer

ABOVE Kuma, Abigail's Siberian Husky, enjoying
the last winter snow in southern Colorado
Contributed by Abigail LaFleur-Shaffer

LIVING AMONG WILDLIFE

Your vigilance is the most important thing to bring with you on a trip. The dangers that humans can encounter are also threats for dogs. The wilderness is overflowing with nasty surprises if you're not well prepared. Wild beasts, toxic plants, and waterborne diseases could harm your dog if you don't take precautions.

Abigail prioritizes Kuma's welfare above all when they venture outdoors. "His safety is just as important as my safety," she explains. "Usually I'm only concerned about wildlife because Kuma enjoys chasing other animals and that could get him hurt. I always bring his leash, and we use an off-leash collar that has different pitch sounds that tell him when to come back to me." But in case something does happen, Abigail always keeps a doggie first-aid kit on her. In fact, the very first thing you can do before bringing your dog into the wild is to get advice from your vet. That way, you'll be prepared if something goes wrong and know how to sense signs of pain, thirst, or fear. Your vet can even help you assemble an efficient first-aid kit that's lightweight but still allows you to respond to most situations.

The Leave No Trace principles apply equally to people and pets: they consist of protecting nature by "teaching and inspiring people to enjoy outdoors responsibly" says the Leave No Trace Center for Outdoor Ethics. While Abigail is extra vigilant about the dangers her dog might face in the wild, she also cares about preserving nature and encourages others to make sure they pack dog poop bags and throw away used bags in the trash—even if that means carrying it for the rest of your trip. It might sound trivial, but any nature buff would agree: "It isn't cool when you're hiking on a beautiful trail, and there's a nice one left in the middle of the path. Have respect for others on the trail," says Abigail.

FROM DOG TO NIGHT

If you're backpack camping, packing light is important, but where food is concerned, there's only so much room for negotiating weight. You want to be smart but not miserly on your dog's sustenance. For Abigail, the balance involves taking "lightweight food and lots and lots of treats." Saving a little weight on one of these will reward both your shoulders and your dog. Besides food, giving your dog clean drinking water is also vitally important, so never forget a water bowl and a water purifier or filter. The risks of waterborne diseases are real; always treat your dog's drinking water unless it comes from the tap or a bottle.

Right now you might be thinking that hiking and camping with a dog is too demanding. But it's really not, as long as you follow this simple advice: *What I have to do for my dog is what I plan to do for myself.* However, if you want to get accustomed to camping with your dog, just spend a few nights in your backyard a few weeks before your hike. Moreover, you don't have to go far and long to make it worthy. A weekend trip also sounds like a good plan. Your first few trips might be better with a car nearby, so you and Rover don't have to haul everything at once.

When it comes to setting up camp and getting some well-deserved rest, a one-person tent might work, but it could be a little bit tight. Before you decide on a tent, take a good look at how big your dog really is. Whatever you choose, your furry friend should always sleep inside with you so he can stay safe and "keep your toes warm"–just as Kuma does for Abigail.

When the night comes after an active day of hiking, you can be sure you'll sleep well. Your dog will, too–even if it's his first time out in the wilderness. As Abigail explains, "Honestly, I don't think there is much difference in the way Kuma sleeps outside versus inside. I think he's different in general in the outdoors versus indoors–he seems more alive and happier outside. But he sleeps the same in either place."

Kuma and Abigail settling in to their campsite
Contributed by Abigail LaFleur-Shaffer

Follow these basic guidelines, and hiking and camping with your best friend can be an immense pleasure–for both you and your dog:

- Find trails where dogs are allowed
- Consult with your vet in advance
- Be attentive to your dog's needs
- Respect nature and Leave No Trace

FOR COMFORT'S SAKE

When Leslie and Connor Gould embarked on Camp Brand Goods, their camping essentials company, in 2011, they wanted to help campers create an inspiring environment where they could revel in nature just as they love to do. For them, camping is more of a mindset than a discipline. A discipline is rigid, governed by rules. For this couple, the only rule that applies is that of enjoying the pleasures of a night or weekend outdoors–in comfort.

Leslie and Connor advocate a pleasant approach to camping, one that's grown on them over years of weekends spent hiking the trails in Calgary, Alberta. They used to prefer a more adventuresome approach, where they'd lug all their equipment on their backs for long days on the trail. Only in recent years has the car gradually come to play a role in the journey–at which point the trunk replaced the backpack, and words like "cozy" and "comfort" became necessary descriptions of any new gear they acquired.

So a few years ago, Leslie and Connor bought a Volkswagen Westfalia Camper to serve as their tent, which kept them dreaming day and night all across Alberta. Within an hour's drive of Calgary– where they were born, grew up, and still live–there's no shortage of options for exploring new places. "I think this last summer we slept in our tent more than we slept at home," says Connor.

They primarily gear their camp outings toward the experience rather than the destination. A deciding factor could be a desire to go fishing in an unexplored river or to try new bike trails. Camping is not just about sleeping outside; it's also about what you do during the time spent outdoors–and what you'll remember when you get home. Connor lists them off: "A few good friends in the middle of nowhere, the shining sun, rinsing yourself off in a chilly lake or stream, late nights around the fire."

"Our camping
trips are usually
as much about
the journey as
the destination."

PREVIOUS AND THESE PAGES
Enjoying all the simplicites of
the outdoors at Two Jack Lakeside
campground, Alberta
Contributed by Mike Seehagel

Leslie and Connor generally prefer exploring new spots–even if it means occasionally ending up in some unappealing dead end or figuring things out as they go along. "We found our favorite spot by scouting backcountry roads on Google Maps." But their go-to trip is a nice weekend at the Two Jack Lakeside campground near the town of Banff. Even if it's not the quietest or most low-key of sites in Alberta, they're always excited to set off there via Highway 93 through Kootenay National Park, or by turning off Highway 40 in Kananaskis. The road offers a range of scenic landscapes that makes the perfect opening for your weekend camp. After all, it doesn't really matter where they end up, as long as they've got all their little necessities in their truck–"including a deck of cards, good food and drinks, and our two dogs, Brutus and Otis."

Napsack moments

ABOVE Contributed by Zachary Nigel

OPPOSITE Contributed by Luc Gesell

WAKING UP

Coffee tastes incredible in the outdoors and can give you so much comfort in the fresh morning. But before you can enjoy that cup of joe, you first have to summon the will to wake up and the courage to leave your comfy nest to face the dampness of the dawn. What if you could reach your first coffee from your snug shell? A sleeping bag, down jacket, and poncho in one, the Napsack was born out of Polar Stuff founder Benji Wagner's desire to "inspire people to get out and do what they already love to do." How many times have you set the alarm clock to watch the sunrise but inevitably switched it off once you felt the cold tickling your nose? Making some of the least enjoyable moments in camping more comfortable, the Napsack is one very cool camp hack.

CAMPFIRE COFFEE

1.

2.

3.

4.

Two things go into making a great-tasting cup of coffee. Of course, the quality of your coffee grounds is important. But also the atmosphere that surrounds you can certainly change the taste. Compare sipping coffee on your sofa with drinking it on a brisk morning in the mountains overlooking a lake. While the couch might sound like a nice idea, try the latter and you'll see your coffee does not taste quite the same.

When Robert Christopher and Zach Pecha created Hikers Brew Coffee, their goal was to help people enjoy a warm cup of coffee in the outdoors. No, just because you're not at home doesn't mean you have to sip dishwater in the morning. Even better, they're really bringing gourmet and fair-trade coffee to adventurous outdoors folk with a sustainable sensibility.

Once you have the coffee grounds, all that remains is for you to know how to make it delicious in your enamel mug. Well, it won't always be delicious—let's be honest—but every sip of coffee will be like a pat on your shoulder. Depending on how you'll camp, minimalist or over-geared, you won't have at your disposal the same tools.

Before reading the following coffee-making options, take a five-minute break and grab a cup of joe—you will want one.

1. COWBOY COFFEE

Maybe the most authentic and easiest to make, Western-style coffee may not be the finest coffee you'll drink in your life, but it has one precious quality: it requires only an iron kettle. Bring water to the boiling point and let it cool one minute beside the fire, until it stops boiling. Then pour two tablespoons of coffee grounds per eight ounces of water into the kettle. Let it rest two minutes and stir it up. Let it rest another two minutes so the grounds fall to the bottom of the kettle. Then say *hello* to your friend Joe.

2. PERCOLATOR

This system requires minimal gear and leaves fewer coffee grounds on your tongue than the Western-style coffee. All you need is a percolator, and if you want to make it look more vintage, seek out an enameled one—it won't change the taste, but it will add some charm to your coffee moment. The percolator will upgrade the camp coffee but also requires a bit more time to sip a mug: about ten minutes for the brewing process plus two minutes to let it rest. But it is worth it.

3. AEROPRESS

The AeroPress is a petite coffee maker that's very easy to use and will delight full-bodied-coffee connoisseurs. Less bulky than a percolator, it is probably the most interesting maker for travelers, as it results in a complex aromatic richness closer to espresso. AeroPress coffee is, in a way, the exact contrary to our old good joe. It also requires you to bring along filters or invest in a reusable one.

4. THE VENTURE POUCH

Very useful for lonesome wanderers, the Venture Pouch fits in a pocket and allows you to brew individual coffee portions. After boiling water, you plunge the pouch in the water, either in your pot or directly in a mug or thermos. Look for these in outdoor stores, or online at Hikers Brew Coffee. You can also make it easily on your own by cutting a coffee filter in several pieces. Flatten them out, place one portion of coffee grounds on each piece, then refold each corner on top of the grounds and close tightly with a little string.

CAMPING WITH KIDS

With their wild imaginations and love of huts, adventures, and storytelling, kids are natural campers. For parents, taking their children on a camping trip is like opening a book that reconnects them with nature, where every page is full of discoveries, amusing experiences, and opportunities to develop life skills. The campsite is the place where you can teach them how to put away the screen and enjoy the simple pleasures of the wild. Moreover, where time and money is tight for many families, this accessible experience holds the promise of building great memories and a lasting connection with nature.

Steamboat Springs, Colorado
Contributed by Lindsay Terbosic

CITY CAMPING IN THE ROCKAWAYS

with Kent Johnson

Next time you're thinking of visiting New York City, try sleeping in a tent rather than staying in a hotel. **KENT JOHNSON** loves introducing newbie campers and urbanites to the wonders of city camping—right in the historic Jacob Riis bathhouse on the beach of the country's largest National Park. Not since the early 1900s has camping been such a popular pastime in the Rockaways. He tells us more.

How did CAMP ROCKAWAY come (back) to life?
I had been surfing in Rockaway for a number of years and was always fantasizing about spending the night on the beach so I could take advantage of multi-day swells. There were no hotels out here at that time, so I was stuck with commuting by car or by subway. At some point I came across some old photos of tent colonies on the beach—there were hundreds of tents that families would rent for the entire season. It looked like so much fun, and I started to imagine what an updated version would look like.

What does recreational camp mean at CAMP ROCKAWAY?
We've tried to design Camp Rockaway as a base camp for experiencing everything the peninsula has to offer, from surfing, kayaking, fishing, and bird watching to exploring the shops, nightlife, and art. The camp itself has lots of areas for relaxing and socializing, like a communal firepit for cooking and roasting s'mores, a big tent with picnic tables, a bulletin board, a library, and games, as well as a bunch of shaded areas with hammocks and lounge chairs.

Would you say CAMP ROCKAWAY is a family campground?
The family camping trip is one of the most iconic American experiences, but it's not something that a lot of urban families have easy access to. In the classic version you need a car, camping equipment, and experience. We designed the campground with the urban family in mind. You can get here by public transportation, and you don't need traditional camping equipment, just a sense of adventure and a desire to experience a whole other aspect of New York.

What is the atmosphere at CAMP ROCKAWAY?
Welcoming, comfortable, unpretentious, and relaxing. A lot of the new "glamping" operations around the country focus on luxury and self-indulgence. We've tried to cultivate an atmosphere that fosters a sense of community and allows for guests to connect with family, friends, and other guests. This happens naturally around the campfire in the evenings, at the communal tent for coffee and tea in the mornings, and for special activities like stargazing and fireside chats with park rangers. I think these are the things people remember and value.

Tent at Camp Rockaway, Riis Beach, New York
Contributed by Allan Schoening and Blessing Marie
Contributed by Nyja Richardson

How important is it to have this kind of place so close to big cities?

We've put a lot of effort into engaging with local businesses and environmental organizations with the hope that our guests have an opportunity to experience Rockaway, and to appreciate its unique character and natural beauty. We're big proponents of sustainability, so we do as much as possible with solar—each of the tents has its own solar panel that charges the lights and fans, and our communal tent has a solar charging station for phones and can run our coffee machine and most of our other electrical devices.

Our showers provide five minutes of hot water, so there's some messaging about conservation around water. We also don't provide bottled water, so you need to bring your own reusable bottle that you can refill at our coolers. Waste is a big concern generally, so we encourage our guests to "pack in, pack out," and we organize beach cleanups with the National Park Service.

If we succeed in introducing our guests to the importance of New York's barrier islands and their ecosystem, and to the low-impact recreational opportunities within a few miles of their homes, then maybe we'll have a better shot at preserving and protecting our local environment and the city we call home.

What do you like the most about CAMP ROCKAWAY?

I love the diversity of guests that we have come to the campground. We get people from all walks of life, and there's something about sitting around a campfire and relating the day's experiences and adventures that gets people to open up and connect in a way that might not happen otherwise.

It's great to see people bond over a shared experience. We had a big storm come through the other night, and the next morning, after the sun came out and everyone was having coffee, there was such a sense of community as guests swapped stories about how they felt so safe and dry while the rain and wind passed outside. Almost everyone says they can't wait to come back. To me, that's the best thing I could possibly hear because I know they're going home with a great memory of Camp Rockaway.

> "The family camping trip is one of the most iconic American experiences, but it's not something that a lot of urban families have easy access to."

FEELING LIKE A CHILD AGAIN

To Matt Miller, a campsite looks like a painting that casts light and color on our childhood memories. Everything conspires to create a sort of *Peter Pan* or *Lost Boys* tableau. In his mind, camping is synonymous with the right to have fun like a kid, even if we've gotten older and even if we don't yet have kids.

"When I was younger, my family would always venture into the woods to camp," says Matt, and replicating those childhood experiences is important for him. It's an easy way to stay connected with the magic of our past.

Matt and his friends wait for the weekend with the same excitement as kids in school. It is a release for them when the moment finally comes, and they can all just let their "wild sides take over for a moment." They usually don't need to go far to express it—their camping spots are within an hour of where they live. Their choice of campsite might take them to lakes and state parks, often in off-the-beaten-track places known only to them. Matt loves "going to places where no one else will be." Feeling lost, or at least hidden, is part of the game. That's when the enchantment happens, and the fairy tale begins.

To create the mood, Matt has a few tricks up his sleeve: wrapping the campsite in battery-powered fairy lights, running in the woods in complete darkness to gather logs and make basic furniture like tables and benches. The feeling of being lost in the dark and catching a glimpse of light from the campsite, where you know your friends are, is thrilling. Music is also key, so he always brings his guitar and portable speakers. As Matt says, "Hearing music echo through the trees sometimes gives me chills. There's honestly nothing like it to me."

OPPOSITE AND NEXT PAGE
Just another camp night in
the woods, Tennessee
Contributed by Matt Miller

Warm and welcoming–these two words define the campsite as an outdoor living room. It's an inviting space where you can bond with friends, tell stories, and enjoy simple luxuries like a wool blanket, hot chocolate, roasted marshmallows, a campfire, and going to bed late . . . a festive little space where for a moment all your worries fall away and you feel like a kid again. *Nighty-night.*

Sometimes you might be jolted out of your reverie. Maybe nature calls at the most inopportune moment, and you have to go relieve yourself in the dark of night. Or it starts to rain, and you have to figure out a different way to make a fire. But all of this is part of the adventure. As Matt says, "There will always be hard times in life, but camping has made me see that all you have to do is be willing to work, and those hard times will soon turn to good."

OPPOSITE **Camp at Max Patch, at the border between North Carolina and Tennessee**
Contributed by Matt Miller

CAMPING
CHRONICLES

Sarah Whiteman

Sarah Whiteman

OUR CAMP AWAY FROM HOME

We've been on the road with our three kids for two months. People tell us we're nuts, but no matter how tired we are or how crazy the kids act, we know we have to make the most of our time with them. After all, we only have eighteen summers together. That's a big part of why we're doing this: we want to squeeze in all we can with them. We want to share the experience of camping and traveling.

Our journey began at home in Texas when we made a rough plan to visit the Pacific Northwest. We showed the kids some pictures and talked about what we might do during our summertime adventure. For the peak season, we reserved our campsites at the busy national parks in advance; other places we left a little wiggle room to find a spot upon arrival. From there we relied on travel books and blogs to find out about the activities and hikes we would want to do once we arrived.

Six thousand–plus miles up this beautiful coast and we've now reached Denali in Alaska, which is truly enchanting. We set up camp, opting to sleep in our truck-mounted rooftop tent. My youngest calls it "our home on daddy's truck." We hike from our campground, watch the kids use stones to "take pictures of each other," and talk with them about the plants, mountains, and animals. We cherish our time in nature, leaving behind the electronics to breathe in the mountain air and listen to distant waterfalls. We hope these experiences have a profound effect on the kind of people our kids will become.

Back at camp, life is nothing like our time at home. The kids make new friends, we play cards as snowshoe hares hop around our campsite, we have breakfast for dinner, and we stay up too late because the sky here stays light for what seems like forever. We wake up, hike more amid the grizzly bears . . . we spot lots of mamas with their little ones. We also saw a moose and caribou. My middle child says, "Mama, did you see Santa's reindeer?!" We watch arctic squirrels go to and from their homes in the ground, see incredible mountain views, play in more streams, learn from park rangers, ride scooters, and play cars. We breathe it all in, trying to hold on to all that we can of this beautiful place. Tomorrow, it's a new campsite and more for the kids to explore.

Denali National Park, Alaska
Contributed by Sarah Whiteman

HOW TO BUSHCRAFT

If you Google the word *bushcraft*, you'll find definitions that align it with wilderness survival skills, but ask outdoors expert Michel-John Dalton to explain the practice, and he'll tell you this is a common misperception. Michel-John has his own definition, based on his actual experience in the woods. He puts bushcrafting somewhere between learning and recreation. It's probably the type of camping that comes closest to the idea of outdoorsmanship developed by Robert Baden-Powell, the man behind the scouting movement and the founder of the Boy Scouts. Michel-John explains: "Bushcraft is about using what Mother Nature provides and having the satisfaction of succeeding in fire lighting, shelter building, hunting, fishing, and cooking. It's about learning the landscape and all the different types of wildlife around you. And most of all, it's about rewarding yourself with a tasty piece of meat grilled over the open flames as the sun sets."

Confusing the word *bushcraft* with *survival* isn't exactly wrong, since both involve similar skills and knowledge. The difference is in the purpose. Following Michel-John's definition, bushcraft uses survival techniques to enhance your sojourn so you can be more comfortable and present in the wilderness–as opposed to learning the skills needed only for the purpose of surviving and escaping a dangerous situation.

Overall, bushcraft is quite a traditional style of wild living, accessible to those both passionate about the outdoors and also handy enough to improvise along the way. Naturally, you can find guides, courses, and other information on the Internet to help hone your bushcrafting skills. After all, why wouldn't you want to camp as a way to learn more about nature while enjoying it, too?

"A week of camp
life is worth
six months of
theoretical
teaching in the
meeting room."

—ROBERT BADEN-POWELL,
FOUNDER OF THE BOY SCOUTS

South side of the Bishop's Hat, Austrian Alps
Contributed by Markus Seer

THE CLASSIC
STARTER BUSHCRAFT KIT

A typical bushcraft kit keeps to the basics. You'll often hear the popular phrase "less is more"—in this case that means you want to take less equipment with you and rely more on nature and your ability to improvise.

- A fixed-blade knife
- A well-constructed ax
- A folding saw or bucksaw
- Rope (usually twine and paracord)
- Cookware (water bottles, mess kits, pots and pans, canteens, utensils, etc.)
- Sleeping gear (blankets, mats, pads, etc.)
- Map and compass
- Tool maintenance items (sharpeners and oil)
- Fire-starting materials (lighters, ferrocerium rods, flint and steel)
- A tarp of some kind (usually optional depending on what you're looking to do)
- First-aid kit

Contributed by Marcus Seer

TOP Contributed by Luc Gesell
BOTTOM Contributed by Mia Janik

South side of the Bishop's Hat, Austrian Alps
Contributed by Markus Seer

THE
ADVENTURE

WALKING, ROWING, RIDING, PEDALING, SLEEPING. Then waking up and starting over. Backcountry camping opens up the horizon by allowing you to go farther distances and stay longer outdoors. With your tent in tow, you can travel from one day to the next, just about anywhere you want—on a bicycle, canoe, or motorcycle, or simply in a good pair of shoes.

When you embark on a multistage journey, comfort ceases to be your central concern. A prolonged effort repeated over several days demands the right conditions for rest and recovery, but you have to make peace with the idea of balance. The balance will fall on a continuum somewhere between pleasure and necessity, comfort and discipline. How much room in your pack do you want to allow for your sleeping system? Will you go with a tent or hammock? Hammock or sleeping pad? A sleeping pad or just a sleeping bag? Answering this stream of questions requires knowledge of the terrain and weather and a certain degree of foresight.

The Sanborn Canoe team in Upper Missouri
River Breaks National Monument, Montana
Contributed by Graeme Owsianski

PREPARE YOURSELF

Planning involves choices. Knowing the weather forecast ahead of time or the types of terrain you'll traverse will certainly help you pack–a valuable thing when you have to stuff a week or a month's worth of equipment into a backpack or satchel.

Of course, there's a certain romance in the element of surprise–many of us fantasize about being the "real deal" and being able to wing it and read nature out in the field. Yet it's still necessary to be prepared and set your sights somewhere between the foreseeable and the unforeseeable. There's no harm in checking the weather forecast or a weather almanac, calling local agencies (such as visitors' centers or the parks service), or getting feedback from fellow travelers on blogs and online forums.

Even though travel camping takes more discipline, it doesn't lose any of the pure pleasure that is the very essence of the activity. You'll find more ritual, a refrain you repeat to a beat, alone or with others. Despite a few more rules, it allows you to maximize the charms and possibilities of the outdoors. The adventurers we meet in this chapter tell us how they found the extra space they needed inside themselves as soon as they settled into their tent or sleeping bag. They open up about their steadiness, routine, challenges, surprises, and joys–their camping life.

BACKPACK CAMPING

When car camping becomes less of a challenge, and you find yourself yearning to hit the trail and not turn back in the same day, you're ready to explore backcountry camping. Flee the crowds and venture deeper into nature with all of your essentials strapped to your back.

The more extreme experience of backcountry camping is *thru-hiking* (or *through-hiking*), which is defined as hiking a long-distance trail in its entirety from one end to the other. A successful thru-hike involves completing it from beginning to end within one season. The term was initially associated with the Appalachian Trail, but it has been extended more generally to other long-distance trails, such as the Pacific Crest Trail and the Continental Divide National Scenic Trail in the United States, as well as the Great Divide Trail, which traces the border between British Columbia and Alberta in the Canadian Rockies. There are many other long-distance trails where you can thru-hike and spend long periods of time in the wilderness.

While thru-hiking demands a more professional approach, any kind of backcountry camping starts with having a healthy dose of common sense, curiosity, foresight, and training. It's true that the point of heading out on an adventure is to learn your limits, but careless planning is sure to make you learn those limits much too soon.

If you don't feel ready to thru-hike, or you're just not interested, consider planning a short backcountry hike–you'll find hundreds of trails around the world that can be done overnight or in a few days' time. Two or three days hiking is long enough for most people to be fully immersed in the wild.

A night in a hammock In
Fontainebleau Forest, France
Contributed by Luc Gesell

WET BUT WORTH IT

When the weather changes for the worst, do you turn around and backtrack to comfort and convenience, or do you accept the bad conditions and slog on? That's a choice you'll likely have to make when camping out on a backcountry hike, and it can be the difference between reaching your goal and pushing it off into the future. Of course, when you are in any danger, you have no choice at all, just the decision to keep yourself safe. But continuing on your trip even if it means spending a night in the rain or snow or in a coat of ice depends on whether you can tolerate a little short-term discomfort.

Maximilien Czech and his friends found themselves facing such a conundrum in the Cairngorms of Scotland. When you think of Scotland, the color green might come to mind—and it's true that the Highlands are very lush. But white summits also exist in the northern highlands of the Cairngorm Mountains. Although at a lower altitude and lower temperatures than you'll find in the Great North, these mountains are in no way inferior when it comes to adventures.

THIS PAGE AND FOLLOWING A frozen night at a swamp in Pitlochry, south of Cairngorms National Park, Scotland
Contributed by Maximilien Czech

Maximilien explains: "On our first night in the mountains, we got battered in a windstorm that destroyed our tent—one pole snapped, the pole sleeve ripped, and many pegs got lost in the snow. We felt we had little choice other than retreating after this disappointing experience." There were four of them at that point. Two of them decided to go to a bed and breakfast, while Max and one of his partners, Shaun, decided to stick to the plan: spend their last night on a summit. They were still determined to reach the Cairngorm's summit. So they continued.

"After braving the heavy rain for two continuous hours in near-freezing temperatures, we finally reached the top plateau, which had a lake and was surrounded by a swamp," Maximilien remembers. The spongy ground didn't give them many options for pitching their wet broken tent. But once they set it up, they fired up the stove for a warm cup of soup. "As the sun went down, the weather cleared, and we suddenly witnessed an absolutely gorgeous sunset while wild deer came out of the woods to say hi." The moment, described by Maximilien, was so intense for them that it was only when they were getting comfortable in their fluffy winter bags that they noticed the temperature had dropped significantly.

Early in the morning as they were waking up, the weather seemed to lift along with them. In the time it took them to wolf down a few spoonfuls of porridge, slap on their still-wet clothes from the night before, and fold up the heavy tent that had earlier collapsed on them, the sky had turned definitively blue. Max and Shaun broke camp. They returned to civilization—where their two friends were fresh from a hot shower, a good night's sleep, and a full breakfast. These were comforts Max and Shaun would get to enjoy in turn, with the added bonus of victory: knowing they'd spent that memorable night outside, and with a great story to go with it.

Hammock party in Fontainebleau Forest, France
Contributed by Luc Gesell

CAMPING CHRONICLES

Luc Gesell

FINDING THE RIGHT SPOT

Of course my friends and I would end up hiking. We'd learn a little about the forest—we now know how to identify a linden tree. We might see a red squirrel preparing its breakfast. And we might taste a few wild blackberries, indiscreetly watch a hawk through binoculars, and attend the screeching solo concert of a wild sow at nightfall.

But none of that was the plan from the start, which came together one summer evening. The adventure took form as a simple scheme to spend a night in the woods with our backpacks, hammocks, and sleeping bags. We set a date and finished our beers: *See you August 4.*

That day, we meet up at the train station for a thirty-minute ride, then we walk the rest of the way. The Forest of Fontainebleau, one hour from Paris, France, lives up to its promise, and there are plenty of good spots to camp, but we don't give it much thought early in the day. Around 5 p.m., the

time when the day begins bleeding into night, we size up our options. This spot isn't bad, but it's too close to the trail. This one isn't cozy enough. This one? Not enough trees the right distance apart to hang the hammocks. The search is exciting. It's serious. We take up the challenge as though we're looking for the land on which to build our home. But this is why we came. Exploring takes a good hour. We divide into two groups, then regroup— with nothing to show. Then, once we've made a few concessions, we discover what turns out to be the perfect spot. The spot overhangs the forest with a view that opens on the sunset, with an ideal tree positioning so we could set our hammocks together, well away from the path and with a flat rocky surface to cook and have diner.

Don't worry about never finding the perfect spot— what you find will become perfect once you've decided to set up camp there.

THE BASE CAMP
AS CROSSROADS

When it comes to the world's highest peaks, skill and knowledge are quite often the only reasonable and acceptable things that will ever get you close to the mountain. Non-climbers find themselves relegated to the base. But that's okay—we can't all be summit adventurers. For those of us who don't challenge our mortality, there are still ways we can admire nature's skyscrapers: take a step back, skirt along the sides, go around them. Of course, you won't get the high that comes with altitude, but your eyes will still soak up all the intoxicating beauty of these legends.

From Mont Blanc to Denali to Fitz Roy, most of the earth's highest summits are surrounded by national parks where human activity is restricted. You can't walk just anywhere or sleep just anywhere. Fine. But luckily for us, pathbreakers and environmental experts have sketched out legal hiking trails in these enclosed protected areas, punctuating them with camping areas that respect the wildlife. That was how my wife, Fanny, and I were able to discover Mount Fitz Roy—which sits between Chile and Argentina—and measure its immensity with our own eyes.

Fitz Roy itself is a magnet that attracts a lot of attention. All along this hike you know that it is up there—so far up that it might as well be in another world—and you can't help but check out each clearing, each opening between branches, to try to catch a glimpse of it. You'll have to wait. The first day of hiking, from El Chaltén to Laguna Torre, will take you several hours. At the foot of this glacier lake you'll find the De Agostini base camp, one of the rare areas around the mountain where camping is permitted.

At the El Chaltén exit, along the first stretch of trail, a ranger station welcomes you and asks what your plans are for your visit. There's no chance of cheating here; everyone must sleep in the prescribed area. While on the first day, the shadow of Fitz Roy's foothills may block your view of the skyline, De Agostini appears as a real turning point in your hike. Tomorrow, your camp will perch at the foot of the mountain. Passing by this waypoint is practically obligatory, so set up camp and enjoy the ambience.

The base camp itself isn't particularly exceptional. The trees completely mask the view of Fitz Roy. But here you're at the gateway to the Patagonian giants, at the crossroads of Cerro Torre and Mount Fitz Roy. Climbers and mountaineers call this home. You'll see some coming back exhausted in the evening and others raring to go at dawn. Hikers may want to stop there just to observe and meet these passionate adventurers to get a taste of their fascinating world. Once you're set up, head down to the glacier beach at the foot of the lake to sit and enjoy the view.

Tomorrow, you won't reach the summit of Fitz Roy, but this night spent at the gateway will propel your imagination to a world more intense than you've ever experienced. But instead of continuing to ascend the mountain, you will follow the trail track and finish the loop to El Chaltén in few hours. However, if things are going well, why not stay one more day? You will have time to read your book, write in your journal, or just admire tirelessly the glacier, just as Fanny and I did for the single night we spent there. And if you're feeling bold, you might approach an alpinist who is just returning from the mountain for a description of the spectacle.

Camping sites like this one are not just grounds prepared for sleeping; they also act like a platform at a train station, holding you back for a short time before you're transported toward your destination—wherever that may be.

THRU-HIKING

In this interview, **CLINT "LINT" BUNTING**, a member of the super-elite club of "triple Triple Crowners"—having hiked the three major U.S. trails in their entirety three times each—explains the importance of training, weight, planning, humility, food management, equipment (at least somewhat), and freedom.

How long would you spend hiking on the Appalachian Trail or the Pacific Crest Trail?
I've now hiked nearly 30,000 miles on the long trails of North America, including end-to-end hikes of the Appalachian, Pacific Crest, and Continental Divide Trails . . . three times each. A thru-hike takes anywhere from three to four months for me, depending on the route. The longest time it's taken me to hike the Appalachian Trail was four and a half months, and the fastest was eighty-six days. For the Pacific Crest Trail, I generally finish in four months, although I've completed it in just over three before. Many variables come into play when embarking on an adventure of this magnitude, and the length of time needed to accomplish this huge mileage fluctuates.

How do you pack your stuff?
I carry all the gear I need from start to finish, resupplying on food and water as I go. Water is easy, since it flows nearly everywhere.

Sometimes it's as far as thirty miles or more between sources, but I plan accordingly and carry what I need. I generally carry a hundred miles of food at a time, which translates into three days. The long trails in North America sometimes route directly through towns, but most often you have to hitchhike at a road crossing into town to restock food, then back to the trail.

I'm a huge fan of ultralight backpacking, which means my base weight—everything except food and water—is around six pounds. This is often viewed as ridiculously light by most hiker standards, but after all the time I've spent outside I've honed my gear down to the bare essentials. I carry everything I need to be safe and comfortable in the wilderness for months at a time . . . and nothing more.

I don't recommend someone jump right in to this style as a beginner. But I do recommend folks get their base weight down to ten to twelve pounds and then experiment as they become more proficient with outdoor wilderness travel. I meet so many people overburdened with enormous backpacks who are suffering during their hikes, and I wish I could help them all lighten their loads. Unless you are traveling in an area that specifically necessitates heavy gear, there is no reason to plan for every single contingency your brain can fathom.

Do you experience weariness after spending a few nights outside?

During the first week or so outside, my body slowly adapts to the rigors of long days on trail. I try to hike only 25 to 30 miles a day while my body adjusts to the routine for that initial week. Feet toughen up, muscles awaken and remember their job, and my brain falls into a slower beta rhythm of mobile meditation. The modern pitfalls that plague our culture slowly fade away, and the patterns of endurance hiking become routine. After that first week or so, my body is fully adapted and I crank up the mileage to 35 to 40 miles a day. Then I don't really experience any weariness that a good night's sleep doesn't fix. If my body does call for a break—and it sometimes does—I'll take a day off in town. Spending a full day in the comforts of a hotel room, feet elevated and a constant supply of delivery pizza, can do wonders for the spirit.

How do you handle food?

If the town my route takes me through has a grocery store, I like to purchase food from them, since it supports the local economy and allows me to sample various foods as I go. When there is no grocery store, I mail myself a cardboard box containing food ahead of time, to be picked up when I arrive. One thing the U.S. does extremely well is the postal service! For a nominal fee, they will ship a box anywhere in the country, which makes obtaining more food easy.

Years ago I switched to a "cold soak" [cooking] method where I merely add water to a small plastic jar of food and allow time to rehydrate my meals. It takes two to three hours to fully rehydrate a meal, but this way I don't have to carry heavy cooking items and never have to worry about starting a forest fire! I can also eat as I hike, if the mood strikes me.

Any advice for future thru-hikers?

Education is key! Learn from the mistakes of others! Realize that a thru-hike is *very* different from a weekend hike, and what you think you know about backpacking is most likely antiquated and unhelpful. A thru-hike is different from anything you have ever set out to do, and failure to prepare yourself can be catastrophic. I highly recommend reading the books *Trail Life* by Ray Jardine, *Backpacker Long Trails* by Liz Thomas, and *Trail Tested* by Justin Lichter. There is a lot of online information as well, but it can be difficult to cut through the nonsense and get to actual knowledge from seasoned thru-hikers. As with anything else online, there is much ignorance disguised as experience!

LINT'S THRU-HIKE ESSENTIALS

Check out his website (linthikes.com) for a full gear list.

- Some sort of shelter
- A warm quilt
- A sleeping pad to prevent heat loss
- Enough clothing to stay warm
- Cooking equipment
- Maps
- Compass
- A trusty umbrella

Taking a few minutes at the Grand Vignemale
Peak, French Pyrénées Mountains
Contributed by Luc Gesell

Breakfast in the back of a truck
Contributed by Wade Montpellier

COOK MEALS IN NATURE

However you choose to camp, at the end of the day, no outdoor enthusiast should go to bed unhappy about their meal. Whether you are in the mountains, along beaches, or in the deserts, enjoy these tips for when you have to cook with limitations.

TINFOIL TECHNIQUE

If you're taking a cycling or hiking trip, you won't be able to pack too many kitchen tools. But you may have the option to light a campfire. In that case, plan a few tinfoil meals, which are a great opportunity to enjoy flavorful meals without having to play chef on site. Prepare the meal at home before you go, and assemble everything in foil that you can just throw on the fire.

IDEA: *Stuff a potato with garlic, parsley, mushroom, and bacon—thanks to its grease you don't need butter. Or wrap an ear of corn in the foil, simply like that.*

This technique will also please the forager cookers who plan to catch a salmon to smoke. Cooked this way, the fish stay juicy inside and tender outside.

IDEA: *Stuff a fish with slices of lemon, herbs, vegetables, and sea salt.*

COOKING WITHOUT WATER

It's not very pleasant, but sometimes—in mountains, on walls, or in deep forests—you won't always have a source of water for filling a pot and boiling, so you may have to rely on what's in your flask. The best idea here is to bring complementary food that you can easily soak and soften. This may not sound like a feast but I promise you'll feel like Tom Sawyer emptying his pockets of treasures after a day of wandering.

IDEA: *Mix dehydrated sweet potatoes (look for these in Asian supermarkets), hard cheese, carrots, ham in a can, or dry fruits into a bowl of quick-cooking oats. Add a bit of water from your flask with sugar or salt and let it soak for 20 minutes. To avoid the overdose of oats (which can happen after two meals), bring along some nutritious snacks. And don't forget the dark chocolate.*

COOKING WITHOUT FIRE

You don't necessarily need a campfire to cook in nature; you just need a portable stove. This category opens the door to our dearest pasta, rice, noodles, and other starches you might be craving.

IDEA: *Pour the oil from a tuna can onto your cooking rice for juicier results, or pack some stock cubes to perfume your boiling pasta.*

THE CADENCE
OF BIKE CAMPING

At departure, photographer Gustav Thuesen's bicycle is loaded
with pounds of gear. He takes off from the southernmost point
of Sweden with 1,300 miles before him and ends his trip at
the westernmost point of mainland Norway, with twenty days
of shooting and cycling behind him–including nights spent
outside, amazing captures, a few hard moments, and a lasting
memory. Between start and finish, Gustav experiences both the
ups and downs of any itinerant camping trip.

   Such a journey is a condensed version of everyday life. Your
tent is your home, and this tiny space serves as your kitchen,
living room, or bedroom depending on your immediate needs.
As Gustav highlights, "In a few minutes, I had shelter from the
elements and could enjoy the comforts of a warm 'bed'"–his
sleeping pad. After reflecting a moment, he adds that camping
every day on the go fosters a routine that, somewhere between
all the chores, transforms into a sort of chorus, a comforting
cadence you keep coming back to day in and day out. Find a
supermarket to buy the same nightly feast, made with the same
two ingredients. Unearth the camping spot of the day. Unpack.
Pitch the tent, unpitch the tent. Repack. But when it becomes
a refrain in a daily symphony that involves breathtaking
scenery, making your bed doesn't sound like such a tedious
task anymore.

A bike-packing trip from the southern point of
Sweden to the northern point of Norway
Contributed by Gustav Thuesen

HOW TO PREPARE
FOR A BIKEPACKING TRIP

- Train for endurance and start with weekend trips
- Determine the stages of your trip and the number of miles you'll travel on each leg
- Don't be too ambitious in your daily distances
- Dismantle your bike entirely and learn how to fix it from the road
- Check your tool kit before you go
- Research campsites or potential camp spots to avoid sleeping along the road
- Anticipate everything and every kind of weather
- Plan to be self-sufficient for a few days with enough food and water to get you through

Sometimes camping makes you wonder why you doggedly pursue this unforgiving lifestyle: "sleeping on an uneven surface, not having a toilet or running water, two-ingredient dinners, and the fact that everything is wet and damp." But all this is part of the glorious grind of bike camping that Gustav loves and accepts, because the rest is extremely rewarding. The grueling aspects make him very grateful for the simple comforts of his everyday life back home. What he learns about himself, the extraordinary sense of freedom, and the outstanding landscapes he captures with his camera easily overshadow any unpleasantness.

"Traveling in general helps you get perspective on your own life."

CAMPING
WITH SPEED

With wheels comes the promise of distance and freedom. They change the scale of your itinerant adventures, taking you farther and helping you cross borders between territories. A hundred miles can turn into a thousand miles, and you can easily see and sleep in a wide variety of places in the same trip.

If we admit the saying that the backpack is the adventurers' home, we can also say that your motorcycle, car, van, or truck is your barn. You can store everything you want inside it, and then charge your backpack with the needs of each stage of your adventure. Imagine wanting to go mountaineering and surfing in Canada. With a car, these experiences can be had in the same trip: load the trunk with snowshoes and surfboards, and you have what you need when you get there. Camping with wheels does not always mean more comfort. However, it opens possibilities for what you'll experience.

30,000 miles with a motorcycle on
the Pan-American Highway. Find out
more on page 103.
Contributed by James Barkman

RURAL ROAD TRIPPING

Alex and Francis, also known as @IamNoMad on Instagram, planned a three-month car trip to connect to the wilderness of Canada more deeply—with as few boundaries as possible between them and their homeland. This travel project fit neatly into their vision "to challenge the societal description of living." So they chose to sleep in a tent all along the journey, rather than rent hotel rooms, regardless of the conditions or terrain, "with the intention to explore remote places like Yukon and British Columbia."

No matter what happened, camping was their modus operandi, as they pressed onward toward their destination to get to know their country more intimately. To be clear, this was not comfortable car camping. They faced blizzards, windy shores, burning sun, dirty roads, cold waters—and no matter what, there was no turning back.

Sombrio Beach in Juan de Fuca
Provincial Park, Vancouver Island
Contributed by @Iamnomad_

"Difficult roads often lead to beautiful destinations."

—ALEX MARCOUILLER

THIS PAGE AND PAGE 97 Sombrio Beach in
Juan de Fuca Provincial Park,
Vancouver Island

Contributed by @lamnomad_

Their voyage was all-consuming; their guiding principle: to explore their surroundings more deeply day and night. With this freedom they could reach more remote areas that are probably unknown to the average camper. The tent was their cocoon from which they would emerge to experience the northern lights; encounters with deer, wolf, and bear; secluded beaches and big surfs; the warmth of bonfires . . . in short, their car linked together the wild gems of Western Canada like a constellation of the night sky. And so they explored their homeland, spending a few days at the same spots, taking the time to really explore the place before moving on to the next one.

After driving more than 2,500 miles, they can say they experienced Canada to the fullest. They built their own Canada with incredible memories, new friendships, and unbelievable stories. In the end, each and every place has made them appreciate the simple and easy things that they take for granted in their everyday life.

CAMPING
CHRONICLES

Alexandre Marcouiller and Francis Fraioli

FROM SNOW TO SURFING IN YUKON AND BRITISH COLUMBIA, CANADA

Here we are, in the Haines Pass area, planning a two-day hike to Samuel Glacier. There's no phone reception, the thermometer is down to -15°F with blizzard conditions. We decide to give it a go anyway—what bad can happen, right? We start walking around 9 a.m., heading toward the glacier. We can barely see what's in front of us but manage to navigate with a compass. The hike is extremely precarious—we can't tell if we're going up or down, what distance we've covered. We stay close so we don't lose each other.

There is so much snow, and every step is tiring because our snowshoes can't handle the weight with all the camping and cooking gear. We have no other choice but to stop there and wait for the storm to pass over. As we are setting up the tent, the blizzard is getting worse and worse. We lie down in our sleeping bags in the tent, and everything seems to get better. Being inside the tent, it almost feels like we could be anywhere and the "warm" and comfortable shelter seems to mitigate the extent and impact of the terrible storm outside. It's funny to think that we feel safe and secure in this tiny capsule made of fabric, but we do. We fall asleep with the sound of high winds and emptiness, just the way it should be.

The next morning, we're shattered to see that the storm is still going strong. We pack everything and decide to head back to the car. The problem

"Being inside the tent, it almost feels like we could be anywhere."

is that our footprints have vanished—the wind has blown them away. We're completely lost and walking blindly. Our only hope is that the phone app and compass will indicate the right way. It's an incredibly stressful moment. We just want to find our way back.

To our surprise, the storm starts to slow down after a few hours of us walking in circles. We hear a sound coming from our left side—the highway must be nearby. We find the energy to pick up the pace and make it to the top of a hill. We've made it—the car is only a few

hundred yards away! We sure have learned a lot from this hectic expedition overall, but in the end this episode was definitely one of the craziest memories of our trip across Canada.

We continue our road trip across the country. The temperature is warming up; it's the beginning of spring here on Vancouver Island. We've heard of a surf paradise on the western coast, just northwest of Victoria, located in the Juan de Fuca Provincial Park. It's definitely a bumpy ride to get there, but you know what they say: difficult roads often lead to beautiful destinations. The spot is absolutely outstanding—waves are pumping, and there's almost no one around. We set up the tent right by the ocean and put on our wetsuits. It's surfing time.

The days go by perfectly. We almost feel at home here on Sombrio Beach, surrounded by old-growth forest, hiking trails on the shoreline, and perfect waves. Who would ever want to leave a place like this? We even find a hidden canyon, full of moss, plants, and a waterfall. We glimpse a group of enormous sea lions sunbathing on the rocks. We end every day cooking dinner over the campfire as waves are crashing nearby and the sky is full of stars. We are connecting with what really matters, with nature.

PREVIOUS AND THIS PAGE
Two days hiking in the Haines
Pass area, Samuel Glacier, Yukon
Contributed by @lamnomad_

THE ROOFTOP TENT

Imagine this: A vintage Land Rover fitted with a rooftop tent, scenic landscapes, quiet dirt roads . . . With this dream combination, Bill Neville, the founder at Trekker Adventures, takes you across New Zealand aboard mythic trucks fully equipped with rooftop tents and all the camp gear you need. As Bill says, "Just bring a sense of adventure and a sleeping bag."

At Christchurch or Auckland, Bill has a few trucks waiting for you that go by the name of Edmund, Gus, Bernie, Oscar, Billie, or The Judge. Edmund is a stick-shift puma two-seater diesel Defender 90. Gus, a stick-shift two-seater V8 petrol 110. The Judge, an automatic five-seater 300tdi diesel 110. Each is fitted with a tent on top of the roof rack that you assemble when you're ready to set up camp, with a fold-out ladder so you can climb into bed.

Sunset in Christchurch area, with a view
on Gibraltar Mount, New Zealand
Contributed by Yann Bervas

View of Mount Ruapehu in Tongariro
National Park, New Zealand

Contributed by Guy Hasler

HOW IT WORKS

Rooftop and truck tents are a very practical and romantic way of sleeping outside—a dead-on definition of road tripping. You don't have to worry about sleeping on a wet ground or choosing the most level camp spot. You don't even need to trek all the way to New Zealand to enjoy the experience. These tents are easily found at your local camping supply store or online and come in different models to fit just about any SUV roof—as long as the roof rack is strong—or truck bed. As Bill says, "They are super easy. They take about eight minutes to set up your first time and three minutes each subsequent time."

Before choosing a model you'll want to be sure to check robustness of the tent and its compatibility with your car. To avoid any surprise, Trekker Adventures have partnered with a manufacturer to develop their own model, featuring their own specifications so they can ensure the quality control.

To enjoy fully the camping experience in New Zealand, Bill recommends a full road trip of both the North and South Islands. In the far north, you'll find amazing beaches that aren't crowded; in the south you'll find incredible mountains, lakes, and scenic drives. Be sure to chat with the locals and see where they love to eat and what sites they recommend seeking out. If you don't have a month to explore both islands, I would personally suggest visiting Christchurch on the southern island, then cutting over to Haast on the west coast and driving north to Karamea.

Riding through Riverside
County to Palm Springs,
California
Contributed by James Barkman

James and friends in Alaska,
on the Arctic Circle
Contributed by James Barkman

RIDING THE PAN-AMERICAN TRAIL

with James Barkman

The Pan-American Highway is a 30,000-mile motorcycle and mountaineering expedition, spanning from the tip of North America to the bottom of South America on the saddle of—for adventurer **JAMES BARKMAN** and his friends—a Suzuki DR650. What started as a childhood dream between three lifelong friends developed into a battle plan to not only complete the journey on motorcycles but also climb the highest and most respected alpine peaks along the way, from Denali in Alaska to Aconcagua in Argentina. James spoke with us about how he and his friends spent nine months sleeping outside, with every night leading them closer to accomplishing their lifelong goal.

For those who also have a passion for bikes and a dream of long-lasting adventure, James does not hesitate to say to them: camping is a rewarding alternative to an unlimited budget. If you don't have big money in your pocket, you must know that you will spend most of it on gas and food. If James's friends didn't opt to sleep under the stars, they would not be able to afford a trip like this, because hotels, motels, or any other accomodations solutions would have been too expensive on such a long trip.

Was the harshness of sleeping outside part of the dream?

I'm a firm believer in the idea that comfort is a killer and have learned to love placing myself in challenging and stretching scenarios. I've always enjoyed and preferred to sleep outside under the stars, whether it's in a tent, hammock, or just a sleeping bag and pad on the ground. I think there's an element of authenticity that goes along with camping. It's not always glamorous and it's often uncomfortable, but it's genuine and it's real adventure.

How did you select your camping spots along the road?

The more time you spend on the road, the more you develop an "eye" for spotting prime camping locations. I've learned to spot every dirt trail and path from a mile away. Maps and mobile apps are always a big help to finding spots off the beaten path.

What makes for a great sleeping spot?

It really depends on the area. For example, during our ride through Guatemala, we found a great campsite for the night, only to realize that it was next to an apparent drug operation in a dangerous area. I love the mountains and the ocean almost equally, so my ideal spot would be somewhere in between the two! Having a water source nearby is ideal as well. A beautiful and scenic campsite is always a priority; however, sometimes we find that night catches us, and any spot that feels safe enough must do.

Have you developed a technique over nine months of packing and unpacking every day?
Absolutely. Organization is crucial to working sanely and efficiently. I will admit that it took me a couple months to nail down my process, but nine months later I can dig into my panniers or duffel, grab what I need, and have camp set up in a matter of minutes. Every inch of my moto luggage has a purpose and a place for essential gear that we carry. Depending on weather, it can be a real challenge. Thankfully, my fellow riders and I are ready and prepared to sleep on the side of Mount Denali or in the sweltering jungles of the Americas.

What is your maximum load on your motorcycle?
At the moment, our loaded motorcycles weigh about 550 pounds, give or take. We aren't exactly sure how much weight our bikes can take, but it must be close! Although our gear arsenal is extremely minimal by most alpine standards, it still takes up quite a bit of space and weight.

Once you arrived at the mountains, where did you leave your stuff that you couldn't take with you on the summit?
Determining what gear we need for a specific climb is an extremely calculated process. A few extra pounds can make or break a climb, as we are always working around small weather windows, and every ounce adds up. On previous expeditions, we have crossed our fingers and left the gear we didn't use locked down on our motorcycles, hoping it would still be there upon our return. Ideally, we leave our possessions at hostels or with friends while we are gone. Every mountain is different, so we must always play it by ear.

On Denali Mountain, Alaska

Contributed by James Barkman

CAMPING
CHRONICLES

James Barkman

A MOTORCYCLE MEMORY FROM THE PAN-AMERICAN HIGHWAY

It had been a long day riding through the Nevada desert in the saddles of our DR650s. Each of us had wrecked our bikes at least once in varying terrain, ranging from deep sand to loose rock on steep inclines. Weighed down with all the weight strapped to our bikes, off-roading is not as easy as one might think.

As evening fell, we spotted a rocky butte a ways off the main road, Highway 50, right after Fallon. We cut off on a dirt trail and headed into the desert. We eventually found and established our campsite high above the desert landscape, after climbing a steep trail that gave us a run for the money. The wind howled, and we used dead shrubbery to build a small fire among the rocks that we slept next to. We boiled water and ate a simple meal of ramen and soup.

In a sleeping bag, on a pad for insulation and comfort, and under a ceiling of stars, we fell asleep to the howl of coyotes and were awakened by the sun.

Route 50 in an unknown desert, Nevada
Contributed by James Barkman

STAY EXPOSED

The Motorcycle Bivouac was created by the company Exposed
to serve as a lean-to shelter for bikers. The open-air structure
allows them to spend the night close to their bike while taking
in the pleasures of nature in the purest way possible. Unlike a
closed and sealed tent, the bivouac uses the bike as a stand for
one end of the shelter. As a result, campers still experience the
wind and sounds around them: this is at the heart of a bivouac,
which is French for the temporary shelter that was traditionally
used by mountaineers and military.

Exposed founder Fabian Furrer and his friend Jonas
di Lorenzo traveled by motorbike for a week along the old
Napoleon route through the French Alps, a journey they'd had
on their minds for a long time. The two friends set out from
Lucerne in Switzerland with a rough plan of the mountain
passes they wanted to cross, then they improvised day to day
according to their whims. They would only begin to look for
wild places to camp as the sun started setting. Now Fabian
acknowledges, "It's not always an easy task in Switzerland,
with such a dense outdoors population. There's a Swiss saying
that if you can find a nice, hidden spot to sleep outdoors in
Switzerland, you can do it anywhere." They often had to exit off
the main highway and wend their way through small back roads
in order to find the best spots for wild camping.

"The night when we rode from Briançon south, we decided
to explore a valley along the Italian border. The valley seemed

The bivouac tent system
Contributed by Fabian Furher

"If you can find a nice, hidden spot to sleep outdoors in Switzerland, you can do it anywhere."

—SWISS SAYING

The bivouac tent system folded
up and ready to go
LEFT Contributed by Jonas Di Lorenzo
BELOW Contributed by Justin Stoneham

OPPOSITE Fabian Furher and friends
riding through the Alps
Contributed by Justin Stoneham

pretty wide compared to the steep environment surrounding it and was lined with lots of little streams and rivers. We knew right away that we'd set up camp there, as close to the water as possible." So, as planned, they ended up taking a path that seemed to head in the right direction, but soon they lost track of it. From then on, they had to completely wing it as they guided their old machines through the valley. Since the trail was so unclear, they ultimately had to backtrack.

Doubt equals adventure, and it's in the pursuit of doubt that Jonas and Fabian have experienced their finest moments. "After a few minutes of euphoria, we stopped along a flat riverbank right next to the water. We unpacked our motorcycles and set up our bivouacs. After a bit of hassle, we were rewarded with this gorgeous setting that could not have been more idyllic. We cracked open a beer and started cooking dinner . . . already pumped up for what tomorrow would bring."

Different camp spots from French Pays Basque to Asturias
Contributed by Elisa Routa

CAMPING
CHRONICLES

Elisa Routa

VANLIFE JOURNEYS ALONG THE EUROPEAN COAST

There's a map prominently pinned to one of the walls of the van. The bluish veins of the roads contrast with the spotless white of the wooden dividers we've just repainted. The floral curtains cling to the cotton cord strung across the passenger compartment like a balanced mountain climber purposefully perched between two cliffs. The accordion mirror bobs back and forth in time with potholes and speed bumps, acting like a clandestine passenger playing hide-and-seek in the rearview mirror. The camp stove shyly sits on a shelf until its next use. The kitchenette overflows with precious treasures needed for our frequent journeys: two pots, a pan, forks, knives, spoons, bowls, an eight-liter water jug with spigot, a dish towel. Everything is carefully considered, calculated, conceived, as meticulously as a control freak mom's baby bag. It would be a grave mistake to imagine the owners of this van as messy hippies; there's no place for chaos when you live on the road. A random T-shirt left strewn on the bed simultaneously becomes a hindrance in the bedroom, bathroom, office, and dining room.

Each odyssey has its own ritual and hides its excitement as best as it can. Our van "Nautilus" remembers amazing detours, steep roads, endless breaks, and hapless breakdowns. Every second, minute, day on the road expands in breadth, substance, flavor, and importance. It's

a parallel world in which taking your time is the norm. The Nautilus is a singular nest built for us to contemplate the outside world while fully taking part in it.

We spend our nights hidden between two wheat fields, turning hundreds of pages while reading by headlight, waking up in the stifling summer heat, taking in the fleeting vapor on winter mornings. Every scar on the bodywork of this van bears witness to our treks through Brittany, Navarre, Basque Country, Galicia, and Burgundy. The hardy palms of Asturias have left their claw marks on the windows, sand from Cap Ferret still tickles the undersides of our feet at times, and petals from Île de Ré hollyhocks add mauve and yellow accents to our now-warped flower book.

The Atlantic coast is our travel companion—our favorite, I must admit. It is comforting, a hand on our shoulder, its embrace at times tender, at other times stern. The ocean serves as a needed twist to our on-the-margin habits as nomadic adventurers—it is a familiar outlet, always beckoning for us to return. It's our only point of reference, a venerable red thread like a marabout's. So when I trace my finger along the contours of the map pinned to the wall of the van, when I draw an illusory path, I realize that our playground is as vast as it is mysterious. What will our next scars look like?

The Boundary Waters Canoe Area
Wilderness, northeast Minnesota
Contributed by Graeme Owsianski

RIVER CAMPING

In some ways, experiencing the wilderness by canoe is not much different from by bike or car. Traveling by river is another type of itinerant camping that offers a bit more comfort than hike-in camping; like the trunk of a car or back of a bike, your skiff has more space and capicity than a backpack for hauling stuff. But paddling in an empty canoe compared to one that's full are two different things. And whether you're in a solo canoe or a larger raft, wind and currents can be sometimes your partner and other times your worst enemy.

Whatever your reasons for taking a canoe-camping trip—whether recreational paddling or more adventurous rafting—another level of skills is necessary for understanding how nature's waterways work. You can't go if you are not able to read the river. You are very dependent on your pack, and your pack is very dependent on the wild. If you lose it or get it wet, the journey is over. Make the journey last as long as you had planned. Do diligent research and book your first few trips with experts.

Some portage efforts in the Boundary
Waters Canoe Area
Contributed by Graeme Owsianski

CANOE GETAWAYS

with Todd Randall

A pure love of camping and an annual canoe trip led Todd Randall—with his cousin Zack Fellman—to begin his camping supply shop, Sanborn Canoe Co., based along the Mississippi in Winona, Minnesota. One summer he and his friends had the idea to build their own canoe and paddles, and the Sanborn adventure took off from there. Todd's vision has been to instill the spirit of adventure in others, with the canoe central to the outdoor experience. Here, we speak with him about equipping people to travel down the river and camp as they go.

What does camping represent for you and your brand?

I love camping. For me it represents a lot of things. It's the ideal of testing yourself and your limits. It's the routine of camp. It's living closely with friends, if even for just a few days. It's telling stories and sharing meals. In many ways, it's what I hope my daily life could be.

How does camping allow you to further your adventures?

Whether you are hiking or canoeing, everything you have to depend on is either strapped to your back or nestled in your boat. For that reason, you must be more aware. If you misread the river's current, you may find yourself quite wet and cold and perhaps suddenly missing all your stuff. At home, or in your car, you see [nature] through a frame. When you are camping, there is no separation. You are in the elements. There is only you and the scents and sounds and slow, unmarked passing of time. It's boundless and yet intimate.

What gear do you take for paddling along a river over a few days?

The answer to this question depends a lot on the nature of each trip. Some trips, our goal is simply to set up camp and sit awhile. For these trips, I like to bring everything. I want to feast at meals and be comfortable.

There are other trips, though, where we plan to be on the water the majority of each day . . . I try to pack as little as possible. I bring essentially two sets of clothes. One of these sets is to be worn all day every day. The second set

CANOE TRIP PRECAUTIONS

- Check a current river access map to find appropriate campsites. Riverbanks need to be accessible, flat, and sheltered.
- Share your project with local people to get the latest info and advice about the river.
- Train in advance. Paddling a full day requires solid shoulders.
- Pack your stuff in airtight bags or barrels.
- Always keep dry clothes for the camp.

will always be dry. I only wear it around camp when there is no rain or moisture in the forecast. Otherwise, it is only for sleeping. Each day I put on my day clothes (even if they are wet), and each evening I put on my dry clothes. For sleeping, I love my down quilt from Enlightened Equipment and a simple foam pad under me.

On these sorts of trips, I don't have much space for luxury items. I always allow myself two, though: coffee and my tobacco pipe. I don't think there is much in this world more peaceful than jigging the bottom of a deep hole in search of trout while blowing smoke rings over the water.

What makes a good spot and a bad spot for camping along a river?

I like a relatively sheltered spot on a peninsula. Shelter keeps you out of the wind, and being on a peninsula generally keeps away the bugs, as a breeze from almost any direction will move past your camp. Of course, a low-lying peninsula with stagnant water is still going to have bugs. The worst spot for me is one with no wind breaks near still water. Bugs breed in still water, and a swarm of mosquitoes can ruin a camping trip in a hurry.

What makes camping great for you?

I love the routine. Waking up with the sun to start a fire and set the coffee percolating. Then the simple, gruff morning greetings between friends as we all grumble our way into a new day. I love packing up camp and pushing off onto calm water. The simple repetition as you put your paddle in the water time and again. I love setting up camp in a new spot and finding the perks of our new home. The smell of a freshly caught fish frying over crackling coals. I love telling and hearing stories while sitting shoulder to shoulder around a fire. Camping is great for these things and so many more.

What great river adventure would you recommend?

Our shop is in sight of the mighty Mississippi in Winona, Minnesota. So, I have to say this is a great place to start. You can paddle on stretches of the river so wide you would think you're on a lake not a river. You can also lose yourself in the intimate maze of backwater channels. This river can present some real challenges, though. You often can't see the current, but it can be swift. The river can catch paddlers off guard with its size. What may take just a few minutes by car could take you an hour by canoe. As always in a canoe, you can't paddle the Mississippi if you're in a hurry.

What waterway would you like others to discover?

One close to home I love is the Zumbro River. It may seem quite unremarkable to many, but I love it. I've been within just a few feet of a bald eagle and felt the beating of wings as it took flight. This intimate connection to nature is incredible.

Any other advice?

Quite simply, do it! And when you go, leave your phone at home. Live a few moments at least outside a frame.

Spotting horse riders while paddling
down the Missouri River Breaks
Contributed by Graeme Owsianski

The Klarälven River, Värmland, Sweden
Contributed by Wolfgang Fuchs

SCANDINAVIAN RAFTING

Since 1980, the Swedish company Vildmark i Värmland has offered overnight wooden raft tours down the Klarälven, Scandinavia's longest river, harking back to the bygone era of log driving. This adventure allows dreamers and the nostalgia-minded to plunge deep into Värmland, an expansive wildlife region in western Sweden that borders Norway. Some ten thousand lakes dot this magnificent forest territory; within it lies the historic site of Sweden's log driving industry–a supremely eco-friendly system of transport.

After several centuries of the practice, 1991 marked the end of the log driving era of floating timber downstream from Värmland forests to sawmills and other industrial sites. Two legacies endure: the hard but free lives of the log drivers along the water; and the wooden raft, that half-tent, half-boat vessel that was born of joining logs together and travels in close formation down the region's waterways.

The days of log driving are long over, but it's still possible to experience this adventure in an authentic way. With the help of experienced instructors, you build your own raft, float down the Klarälven, and dip your toes into the water for a voyage you won't forget. You will travel through the outstanding and very quiet forests of the Värmland, stopping here and there along the Swedish river as you wish for a salmon fishing party (you'll need a daily license) or just for swimming. The water is crystal clear and the bathing absolutely recommended. For the night, the Klarälven offers plenty of cozy riverbanks surrounded by pine trees. This is just the adventure that Vildmark i Värmland aims to provide.

THE ART OF

THE CAMPFIRE

Everywhere they travel, hikers, canoeists, and other outdoors types will probably wonder, "Can we build a campfire here?" The question has become a sort of camper's elegy on the outdoors forums and blogs. Even though campfires are severely restricted or prohibited in most nature reserves and in many national parks, the storybook image is one that dies hard. Hanging out with friends or loved ones around the fire in the middle of wilderness at sunset: it's hard to resist. And so the campfire has become a burning if elusive desire for campers.

But the essence of the campfire is actually not just in lighting a fire. There's a reason why hearth and home are synonymous: it's where people gather for warmth when it's cold and gray outside, to chat and tell stories around the fire. The light and flames create an open space for camaraderie and happy memories, from yesterday and for tomorrow.

TIP FOR HIKERS

If you're hiking and camping where campfires are strictly prohibited, bring along a camping stove:

- The collapsible wood stove is very light and compact, as you don't need to bring along fuel.
- The tab stove is heavier, as you have to pack the fuel tablets.
- Gas bottle and its burner is the heaviest solution but better for slow cooking.

HOW TO BEGIN

Be sure you know the current regulations of your campground or park. Even if campfire is not prohibited where you go, it's always better to not light one in dry and windy conditions. Also, if any firepit exists, choose one at a harmless distance from your tent and the trees. Sparks and flames can reduce forests to ashes in just a snap of the fingers. With that in mind, following are a few tips for building a successful and safe hearth.

Prepare the firepit.

If possible, choose a soil or sandy perimeter for your fire unless there's a designated firepit at your campsite. Make sure to clear away any litter or stray grass or leaves near the pit. You don't want your fire to travel. If you'd like, you can dig a hole to protect the fire against wind. Then form a circle with rocks to establish a safe boundary and prevent the fire from spreading.

Pile up some kindling and tinder.

Pile up kindling logs (if you can find some) three by three, on two levels. Six dry and thick logs should be sufficient. (Moist logs will waste all your efforts.) Then fill out the spaces with dry material as tinder: leaves, little twigs, pine needles, and pinecones. You want these dry elements to catch fire first, but they need to be protected by the log structure.

Make a tepee structure.

Find longer twigs and branches and pile them up all around the circle to form a tepee over the kindling logs.

Scratch a match.

This sounds like the easy part, but it can also be hell—don't forget to store your matches in an airtight box so they don't get wet. If you're camping in strong winds, see page 242. Throw your match into the fire rather than tossing it on the ground. The embers on an extinguished match can still start a wildfire, plus there's no need to litter.

For those who enjoy the crackling of a campfire but not that much the lighting process, you must know that fire-starter kits exist. They are a nice sparking tool for your campfire, but don't forget to keep it alive then.

Fuel it up.

Watch over your fire, making sure the flames stay alive, and place a log in the middle of the fire once it's going strong. Be careful to not suffocate the embers.

Always extinguish it.

Never leave a campfire unattended—especially with kids around—as the wind could turn the divine flames into hell. Always make sure to completely extinguish it with water before you retire to your tent and definitely before you leave the site.

CHOOSING WOOD

Keep in mind several criteria when choosing the wood for your firepit. You'll want to find enough hardwood and softwood, as both have their own benefits. Softwood is easier to split and better for starting a fire, since it burns more quickly. Hardwood is more difficult to break and to light, but it burns longer. You'll need some of both.

A few more things to remember: Never pull branches off the trees—there is more than enough wood on the ground. Be careful never to take wood from an animal's shelter. And always check the park's rules about bringing in outside firewood. Learning a bit about nature will help her, and reciprocally will help you.

"It is not a campfire if there are not stories."

—RICK BASS,
THE LOST GRIZZLIES

Twin Lakes, Colorado
Contributed by Lindsay Terbosic

THE
WILD
CHASE

WAVES, GRIZZLY BEARS, SALMON, WHALES, the perfect view—all of these can easily elude the carefully laid plans of surfers, photographers, observers, fishers, hikers, and other nature peekers who head out in search of wildlife.

Getting close requires investing in your relationship with the outdoors. That means listening to nature more closely and making the effort to understand that it does not belong to us; we belong to it. We can surf because the position of the sun and moon gives us the right waves. We can fly-fish because a river's ideal conditions have stocked salmon or trout at the source. None of this just happens with the snap of our fingers, whenever we feel like it. It takes patience, timing, preparation, and adaptation.

MINGLING WITH NATURE

Camping is a tool of patience. For the women and men highlighted in this chapter, it provides time outside, as well as shelter while they wait for nature to unveil just what they set out to find.

To go wildlife watching, you'll need to blend in to the landscape. Your campsite should leave as little trace as possible, both on the ground and in the air–and in the eyes, nose, and ears of the species you're searching for. If you're chasing waves, auroras, or other natural phenomena, your perfect spot is not just a matter of *where* but *when*.

In any case, your ability to stay in the moment is what will make your camping experience more or less memorable.

PREVIOUS Ucluelet, Vancouver
Island, British Columbia, Canada
Contributed by Graeme Owsianski

OPPOSITE Majestic Ural owl
Contributed by Benjamin Kinadeter

HOW TO FOREST BATHE

Urban populations live in a chronic state of stress due largely to the constant connection with technology and lack of access to nature. Fortunately, in the early 1980s, Japanese researchers developed *Shinrin-yoku* therapy, which translates to "immersion in the forest environment," also known as "forest bathing."

But this strange term does not simply imply a walk in the woods (nor does it have anything to do with cleaning yourself). The therapeutic practice demands really *being* there, body and soul. It means switching off your device and plugging in to your senses. Inhaling. Exhaling. Listening. Smelling. Touching. It means taking the time to experience the quiet and stillness of the natural environment.

Humans have always had the intuition that spending time outside—simply walking, breathing, and relaxing among the trees—is good for us. And indeed, scientific studies have confirmed significant regenerating effects on the body, including strengthening the immune system, lowering blood pressure and stress levels, affecting mood, improving quality of sleep and concentration, and even reinforcing relationships. Studies have shown that spending just fifteen minutes in nature has a noticeable positive impact. So imagine the health benefits of a night of camping. After a few days outdoors, the effects nature has on creativity and cognition only amplify.

For generations, the inspiring words of enlightened spirits such as John Muir, Millican Dalton, and Henry David Thoreau have opened the doors and shown the path leading to the great outdoors. Now scientific research only confirms how wise and visionary they really were. If by chance you are reading this and are feeling anxious, and you have no plans for the weekend, I suspect you now know what you can do.

ABOVE AND NEXT PAGE
Forest bathing in Fontainebleau, France
Contributed by Luc Gesell

THE UNSHELTERED

"You can see and hear better without a tent." For Benjamin
Kinadeter, sleeping outside deep in the woods is about
communing with nature, becoming one with it, rather than
escaping to a tent at the end of the day. Placing a piece of fabric
between him and the forest floor would lose the very essence
of camping. "People often ask me if I am afraid to sleep deep in
the woods. Crazy! I can't understand it. I am alone there, and
nobody can hurt me." Listening to Benjamin, you realize that,
for him, you don't sleep in nature; you sleep as one with it. In
this sense, indeed, what is there to be afraid of?

Benjamin likes camping with friends, but he'd rather do it
alone. As it is, there are plenty of new acquaintances to make
in the woods or mountains, as long as you're silent. He doesn't
dislike talking; he'd just rather listen. "You're a different person
when you're alone in the forest. You listen more, you see more,
you smell more, you feel more." In this sense, nature becomes
a different experience. The final hours of daylight are the most
magical, especially the silence. "You should go into the woods
and listen to the birds. A minute after sunset, there's no more
noise, no more birds. It's surreal." The moment the sky turns off
the lights, one part of nature goes to sleep, as another wakes up.

Benjamin believes the point of camping is to be as simple
as possible, so he only packs a sleeping bag, a camping stove
for coffee, a sleeping pad, and some photography equipment.
"I leave my home, my bed, to lie down under a tree." And the
weather, which is sometimes gentle and other times stormy? It's
also a part of nature, so it counts among Benjamin's reasons for
sleeping in the wild. And what about bugs, you ask? You might
be surprised to learn that Benjamin avoids repellent because

Snowy autumn night in Austrian
mountains, close to Obertauern
Contributed by Benjamin Kinadeter

the smell repulses the fauna around him—leaving little chance of spotting wild animals. His best bet is to cover the maximum surface of his body with dark clothes.

Behind these words, Benjamin's idea is obviously not to re-create his bedroom from home in the middle of nature, but to settle down with his surroundings as unobtrusively as possible. His rewards: to see the open sky, feel the cool breeze enter his nose, and hear the birds. To live at nature's pace is the best way to observe life in the wild.

"The essence of camping, in a strict sense, is to sleep within nature, in its midst."

CAMPING
CHRONICLES

Benjamin Kinadeter

A BIRDER CAMP

Birding photography, just like any wildlife photography, is about waiting hours and sometimes days. To give yourself a chance to reward your patience, you'll want to follow some basic advice, courtesy of an ornithologist friend of mine.

As is often the case with wildlife adventures, you first want to gather as much information as you can before going on your trip. Once you know where to go, you need to be very attentive to your approach. The observation does not start after you set up the camp. It starts far before, from the moment you enter the site.

As you enter the area, you want the wind at your back as much as possible. Indeed, because wind carries smells, it is better to not have it blowing your scent where you think the birds are nesting. It's even a good idea to wear the dirty clothes from your previous outdoor getaways. You actually want to smell like the woods. Laundry detergent, shampoo, and even hormones can make creatures scatter.

You'll also need to give yourself time to prepare your camp and settle into your surroundings before you can expect to see any birds. The more you can blend in, the higher your chances for successful observations. Gear plays an important part in this. You may want to invest

in a camouflage tent specifically built for bird-watching; they are upright and include a window, so you can keep an eye on nature with your camera while sitting in a comfortable position. Otherwise, bring a camouflage net.

Now you know how to elude the birds' sense of sight and smell. What about sound? Avoid making too much noise by springing for materials made of wool and cotton instead of synthetic fabric that could make scratching sounds and give up your location to perceptible birds.

These tips do not promise that you'll get to see birds, because even if you master the art of camouflage, birds also have impressive senses. Nevertheless, they can increase your chances significantly.

ABOVE A common bullfinch
LEFT A capercaillie
Contributed by Benjamin Kinadeter

OPPOSITE Tripoint border in Sumava National Park, where Germany, Austria, and the Czech Republic meet
Contributed by Benjamin Kinadeter

"Camping is the space
and time created
in order to enjoy a
moment in harmony
with nature."

A winter morning on Lake Wanaka, New Zealand
Contributed by Johan Lolos

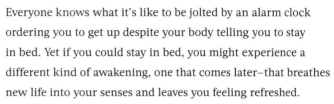

AWAKENING
ONE'S SENSES

Everyone knows what it's like to be jolted by an alarm clock ordering you to get up despite your body telling you to stay in bed. Yet if you could stay in bed, you might experience a different kind of awakening, one that comes later–that breathes new life into your senses and leaves you feeling refreshed.

It's May 2015–the end of fall in New Zealand. The ski resort town of Wanaka wakes up under a dusting of snow. No one's ready. It's too early. But it's time to get up.

Johan and Ben, friends who met in Wanaka, decide to freshen up their senses and get their blood moving by planning a morning camp. There are some who set up camp to go to sleep, and others, like these two, who set up camp to wake up. They have the idea to go camping for just a few hours seeking the warmth of a coffee over the campfire and the early-morning freshness of an overeager winter.

Their day begins the next morning at 6 a.m. While most of their neighbors haven't budged from their slumber, Johan, Ben, and Ben's Alaskan malamute, Maska, head out to chop some wood, as well as punctuate the blueness of this supremely cinematic hour with the help of an ax and some flames. Once on site, Johan observes the pure relationship between his friend, his dog, and nature–no one seems particularly concerned about the cold. A bit more effort, and they'll all be able to nestle into this tranquil little hour, which will gently ease them into the pace of their day. Silence. The fire comes to life. The coffee is ready. They'll each bundle up under a wool blanket and stay put. Then they'll watch and listen.

As Johan recounts this memory at times he seems hesitant: "We didn't really camp. We didn't sleep outside . . . " But camping is the space and time created in order to enjoy a moment in harmony with nature. So I'd say that yes, Johan, camping was a part of your little escape.

CAMPING
CHRONICLES

Lionel Prado

SEEKING NATURE'S CLUES

I walk toward an old hamlet located in the Southern Alps. Farther up, there is a slope where wolves pass from time to time. That's where I'll set up my camp. The temperatures are cold. It's a perfect time for loneliness in these mountains, which exist out of time. My mission for the coming days is to seize the unexpected, to meet the wild inhabitants of this landscape.

So of course, to encounter the unexpected, sometimes you have to know whether to move at the right time or wait in the right place. I choose to wait, to stay put. To not leave everything up to chance, since experiencing the beauty of these mountains stems above all from relentless will. The time that passes slowly sometimes makes you doubt. But waiting is the price to pay for serendipity.

The pine tree I'm camping under provides open-air shelter, but only for a few days. The transition of the first day is difficult; the days that follow, my body adapts. Sleeping here allows me to observe and understand, an essential process that nourishes a beautiful image of nature. The nights are long, and the full moon disrupts my sleep. I start imagining the pack of wolves passing near the camp in nocturnal silence. At daybreak, it's freezing out and hard for me to leave the warmth of my down sleeping bag.

My camp is limited to a well-inflated sleeping pad, a sleeping bag, four days' worth of food, and my photo equipment. In the hollow of the pine lies my notebook, where I record fragments of life, my thoughts and observations. Four days in the snow is the time it takes for nature to start delivering snippets of its secrets—for it to begin letting you into its privileged realm.

At first the landscape is empty. With patience, ermines, partridges, and grouse make their presence known, to the great pleasure of the dreamer who can contemplate without disturbing them.

The ermine is fast and silent. It is better to be awake for his furtive passage, even if it means waiting for chance to occur.

The sun illuminates the summits; my spot remains in the shade. While I'm still in my sleeping bag, the ermine suddenly emerges. I did not expect it. This is our chance encounter. This is the moment that surprises and amazes.

PREVIOUS A chamois met in the Mercantour National Park, French Alps
Contributed by Lionel Prado

ABOVE A curious ermine watched by Lionel Prado
Contributed by Lionel Prado

RIGHT Minimalist camp in the Mercantour National Park
Contributed by Lionel Prado

Campground at Mer et Monde,
Grandes-Bergeronnes, Quebec
Contributed by Luc Gesell

WHALE WATCHING IN QUEBEC

"This is a nature reserve. Not SeaWorld." All it takes are these few words from a local guide for Fanny and me to understand. We came to the banks of the Saint Lawrence River to camp and whale watch by canoe, rather than motorboat. Then it hits us: there are whales here, and we may get to see some. But it's not our given right. She hastens to add, ironically, "The Beluwaves, however, will escort you along the entire Saint Lawrence."

Beluwaves? That's the lingo (also known as *Beluvagues* in Québécois) for describing the imagined sight of a beluga, a small humpback whale whose milky color blends conveniently well with the sun's reflections dancing on the waves–*vagues*, in French–of the Saint Lawrence. The possibility that we'll succumb to this mirage gets a little stronger when our guide warns us that there are only 300 specimens of this particular population of beluga whales left–in all of the seas and oceans combined. On the Whale Route, they are a driving force, but we may have to find inspiration elsewhere to sustain us as we progress on this path. We've come so far to camp along the shores of the Saint Lawrence and watch the belugas, with distance and respect. But we've been warned that it might not happen.

The local population has turned the Whale Route into a tourist and economic hub. From crafts for sale to hotel decor, everything is whale themed. Our bus is heading toward the Grandes-Bergeronnes, our observation point. As we move north,

the immensity of the geography dwarfs our dreams—of course, we continue to believe we'll get to see the whales breaching loud and clear before our eyes. But, of course, we're not at SeaWorld. The bus stops on a corner of the road. The driver yells, "Grandes-Bergeronnes!" That's our cue; we rush to grab our bags in the hold. No sooner does the bus start up again and disappear behind a curtain of dust. Here we are, at Mer et Monde, our camp spot. Time to settle down for a few days, set up our observation post, and explore the area.

We get lost in the pines—in fact, we are on a marked trail, but we like to think we're going deep into the woods, to the unknown. We find the camp spot we booked already set up with the canvas tent, and drop our bags; we're struck by the tranquility of the place. We grab our binoculars and a thermos, and off we go. A few minutes of peering through our binoculars, and already we're antsy. That's it for the day. Patience now gives way to the warm excitement of returning to camp. Back at the site, we boil water and cook a light dinner: soup and crackers, plus a bit of chocolate for dessert that pairs nicely with our warm tea. The sun sets, making way for the stars. Frost sets in overnight. We think, maybe we'll have luck tomorrow.

Kayaking and whale watching on the Saint Lawrence River, Quebec
Contributed by Luc Gesell

Things are looking up the next morning. A powerful geyser of saltwater from the river startles Fanny. The cold of dawn is rapidly warming up. The rest of the day will slide back toward sweet new disillusion. No bitterness though; this is the game. And these are the rules we have accepted: sleeping along the Saint Lawrence, turning in and getting up in time with the sun, taking our time rather than drowning our days in a fantasy boat that sprints zealously toward the whales in total disregard for their tranquility.

Nine times out of ten, those who camp along the Whale Route come back empty of whale tales to tell, but instead have an inspiring morality tale: We do not rule nature. When visiting, we respect our wild host, which is already so generous. Nature is there to learn from, to understand. But nature takes its time.

FISH AND PITCH

Remove but not impoverish. That's the fishing philosophy
of Graeme Owsianski, who lives in the heart of Vancouver
Island's wilderness. For him, the pleasure of fishing lies in
approaching nature, always respecting the way fish fit into the
greater ecosystem. Of course, catching fish is the goal. Actually,
catching *one* fish is the goal—one fish to grill over the fire for
a delicious wild dinner back at camp. One is enough—just
one pink or coho salmon will do the trick. Yet 95 percent of his
fly-fishing is purely and simply catch-and-release. Remove
but not impoverish.

Fishing is like a blessing: "Covering new ground, heading to
new spots . . . fishing can take you to some of the most beautiful
and pristine areas imaginable," Graeme says. Fishing trips
usually require some planning, and his work starts the night
before. Tying flies, researching locations, checking the weather,
and organizing gear takes some time, and dawn is not far off. By
the dock, the shore, or the road, Graeme and friends are ready
in the early-morning hours to head out to their chosen spot on
a river or beach. Getting there can take hours. Being prepared
and equipped to camp gives them the opportunity to cover
much more ground amid the network of waterways. It doesn't
matter whether it's a newfound spot or one of their old classics;
once they've settled on it, it becomes the perfect spot.

"Once you're there, it's completely calming. For me,
there's nothing like standing in the middle of a river with water
rushing around you in the middle of nowhere. Casting and
being in that setting becomes meditative. Hiking and wading
down a river offers a completely different experience that most
people don't ever think of." Graeme remembers a particular
trip early one September. "The coho fishing was incredible off

Fishing for coho in the heart of the Vancouver Island wilderness

Contributed by Graeme Owsianski

"A fresh-caught salmon cooked over the campfire is one of the simplest but most wonderful pleasures that life has to offer."

the beach and at the river mouth. You couldn't keep them off the lines, and getting to keep a choice one for dinner while camping—it doesn't get any fresher." To Graeme, a fresh-caught salmon cooked over the campfire is one of the simplest but most wonderful pleasures that life has to offer.

Camping allows you time during those early mornings and late evenings when the fish are most active, when they rise to the surface to feed. You can slow down and begin to study what they're feeding on; you can take note of the caddisfly or insect hatch that may be occurring, which determines what fly you pull from your tackle box. Camping allows you to fully immerse yourself in the art of fishing.

The more time you spend wading through the water, the more the river ecosystem splashes to life. Watch the salmon return to spawn as they fight their way back upstream. Observe the eagles and bears lining the shore waiting for their part in this circle of life. These are special moments, and you are part of it all—not as a river thief, but as an organic link in the chain.

Camping and fishing this way create a strong bond that will stay with you long after you head back to civilization. Close your eyes and you can imagine it. Graeme paints the picture: "Standing among the towering giant trees of the watershed that has benefited from the salmon returning to the earth along the shoreline . . . It's humbling."

Preparing freshly caught
salmon for the campfire
Contributed by Graeme Owsianski

NEXT PAGE Fishing for coho
in the heart of the Vancouver
Island wilderness
Contributed by Graeme Owsianski

"Go with surf in mind,
but stay open-minded
to fishing, hiking,
exploring, and other
camp activities to
keep you busy or let
yourself relax."

Hunting winter waves in Vancouver Island
Contributed by Graeme Owsianski

CHASING WAVES

Logging has already largely devastated many wild places on Vancouver Island. On the one hand, this has had the effect of offering greater access to outstanding wilderness to more people. On the other hand, it has put stress on the surrounding area, watershed, and inevitably the salmon habitat. This is the paradox between our strong urge to protect nature and our equally strong desire to explore it. How do we strike a balance?

In fact, you can enjoy nature and play by its rules by being grateful for what the great outdoors offers, whatever the weather or how you get there. As Graeme explains, a secret surfing spot where he likes to camp involves traveling possibly perilous conditions. "Getting there takes time. For myself, that's a six-hour drive to the north end of Vancouver Island, and then a two-hour drive on an active logging road. If there weren't logging roads, you wouldn't be able to access this place. With active logging happening in this area, you're on 'their' road–with oversized, fully loaded logging trucks that aren't stopping or making way for you. So proceeding cautiously is crucial. If an accident were to happen, not only would it end in quite possibly a terrible outcome, but also the logging company could easily put up a gate and it would all be over for everyone." Fair warning, but understand that Graeme isn't even close to his end point yet. Like the famous saying, this spot is clearly as much about the journey as the destination.

At some point Graeme has to leave his truck on the side of the road and continue on foot. Several options present themselves. He could choose a grueling hike with all his gear on his back while lugging his surfboard in his arms along a daunting muddy trail. Canoeing is the second option, and the one chosen by Graeme and his friends. The reasons why may seem obvious.

First of all, "you are paddling down an absolutely beautiful watershed." It also gives you the ability to load your skiff with all the gear you'd need to set up a proper camp (tarps, tents, and cooking materials). Plus, there's always room to throw in a fishing rod–maybe even a collapsible crab trap–ensuring you'll get some fresh delicious meals. A chainsaw will definitely be your friend up there too: the beach is an endless driftwood reserve, and being able to cut up firewood at will is great for making a campfire. And thanks to the canoe gods, you could even haul a case of beer without breaking your back.

Paddling to surf in a secret spot, to the north end of Vancouver Island
Contributed by Graeme Owsianski

"It is not a difficult river to navigate, but timing it with the tides is to your advantage," Graeme explains. It's not so much a race against the elements here; it's more a game in which you have to play by nature's rules. "Entering at a high tide, slack, or just on the ebb makes the journey to the ocean easy. You go with the flow with little paddling. There are some large trees that have fallen across the river that you might have to navigate around, or hump your canoe over on a lower tide—there's been a couple notches cut in them to make it a little easier. When leaving, you want to time it on a slack tide or on the flood, since paddling against the tide and flow of the river becomes an instant struggle."

Surfing is the motivation for the trip, but it's far from a guarantee up here. Even though Graeme sees this remote beach as one of the most beautiful places on earth, he won't hesitate to stare the ocean down and . . . let that fickle beast win. Anyone headed here to surf should be prepared for this same sort of reality check: there is no guarantee that the ideal surfing conditions will line up. But it would be a waste to wallow in disappointment just because your surfing dreams were dashed. "Go there with surf in mind," Graeme says, "but stay open-minded to fishing, hiking, exploring, or other camp activities to keep you busy or let yourself relax. And know that you won't be interrupted by any notifications on your phone."

Whatever the adventure there ultimately brings, the chase is worth it. More than just a surfing destination, it is also a terrific wild camping spot. But by "camp," think beyond the tent—it's a place where you can have a truly authentic outdoors experience. As Graeme says, "It's just as much about the trip getting there. You have to put in the effort. It's a long drive to the middle of nowhere, with the nearest town two hours away and no cell service. It's getting off the grid that immediately eliminates most of the distractions of day-to-day life. And you're left with peace and quiet, surrounded by the incredible nature that is the rugged west coast."

THIS PAGE AND FOLLOWING
Camping and surfing in Graeme's secret spot
Contributed by Graeme Owsianski

"A big part of why people camp is because they want to have a place of their own for a while."

Surfing trip in Lofoten Island, Norway
Contributed by Roman Königshofer

SLEEPING ON THE BEACH

with Roman Königshofer

ROMAN KÖNIGSHOFER lets us in on his surf trip to the Lofoten Islands, Norway, where he and some friends chased waves while overnighting on the beach. His passion for natural light and offshore winds, deep powder and tall peaks, motivates him to get out there in search of stories to tell. Living outdoors makes life a story in itself. Surfing and camping come together as one to elevate the authentic emotions life can offer.

Where did the idea for this trip come from?
We went to the Lofoten Islands in May 2016. The weather was crazy! We had everything—sun, storms, rain, snow, winds, and so on. I think that also was what made this trip so special. It was actually spring but felt like that just two days max. I don't know the exact temperature, but it did snow.

I was joining my friends, who were already on a long trip around the whole Baltic Sea for two months. I was with them a little over two weeks, and we all spent just one week on the Lofoten. We had a schedule and couldn't spend more time there. But this week was intense.

To be honest, we decided spur of the moment to drive there, since the original plan was to explore the Baltic Sea. I flew into Helsinki, where my friends picked me up. At that time there were no swells/waves in sight for Finland. So I told them we should just go to the Lofoten. An hour later, we were driving for twenty hours straight up north. Everyone was in good spirits, and it was so exciting! Arriving in the middle of the night on the Lofoten was really special. It was snowing there!

In those conditions, how were the nights and mornings?
Ha ha—that's a funny one! Well, it's sleeping—not much different from at home in your bed. I mean, as soon as you fall asleep, you sleep. But everything before and after is definitely different. After surfing and freezing all day, you just enjoy the warm sleeping bag and sleep as deep as you can. Hopefully there are waves the next morning—you always hope for good waves. The nights were okay. Two slept in the car and two in the tent. We had good sleeping bags. Getting up in the morning and into the cold, wet wetsuit was the worst, though.

How was it falling asleep in a tent to the sound of waves?
It's cool. It's always good to hear waves. That's what you want—that's what you're here for. But it's way more exciting in the morning, because you are frothing for the next surf session.

What gear did you take with you?
We had a basic mattress in the car and two sleeping bags. In the tent we had two air mattresses and two sleeping bags as well.

Were you camping for pleasure, or as a means to the end of wave hunting?
Both! It was a real pleasure, a beautiful place to be. Camping right at the waves is the best you can do— as soon as it is on, you jump in. . . . And if that means it's at two in the morning, you just do it. At that time of year, it doesn't get dark up there. So more time and opportunities to catch good waves.

I love the camping lifestyle. It brings you back to the basics—just your friends and you! No schedule. Just surfing, cooking, eating, shooting, sleeping. So many good things come with camping. And it's dirt cheap—no rent to pay. It's a more authentic experience.

What about cooking?
We always cooked inside the car. On the floor. We crammed four guys into the bus and cooked food for ten people and ate it all every day! Surfing makes you hungry. And surfing in the cold makes you even hungrier. So the biggest issue always is to get food from a supermarket when you are in such a remote spot.

What makes a campsite unforgettable?
No crowds! That is all. A big part of why people camp is because they want to have a place of their own for a while. And of course, having good company—people are everything. Sharing the experience with your friends is the best. Smiles all day long!

This Lofoten trip was definitely a highlight, and it was also not the last time. Everything just fell into place. The crew, the spots, the spontaneity . . . it was such an adventurous trip. I loved it!

A 1984 Toyota Land Cruiser drove them from one spot to another.

Contributed by Roman Königshofer

THE HIDDEN SITE

Jamie Justus Out just saw a photo of the place, but he
knew he had to experience it for himself. Yet it is a closely
guarded secret, and he knew getting there would require
enormous respect for the local people and for the places
they rightfully protect. Nobody will just tell you where
it is. You have to talk to people and draw it out of them,
cross-checking the information from some, accepting the
silence of others, promising to keep the secret safe.

"There were no guidebooks or information on the
Internet about the location, so I had to ask some locals
if they could help me out. A lot of them were hesitant
because they are very protective of their spots, and I
promised I would not share the exact location," Jamie
confides to us. Of course, Jamie wouldn't reveal the exact
spot, but he did hint to this enchanting place being located
in the great somewhere on the island of Oahu, Hawaii.

The real challenge in reaching this site lies more in the
marathon of unveiling the secret, since the hike took only
two hours to reach the tiny camp platform. Which doesn't
mean it was a walk in the park. "The ridge hike to get there
was a little perilous at times," Jamie says–which isn't so
surprising when you plan to camp perched on the edge
of a pretty big drop-off. Once he and his brother-in-law
got there, the magic set in right away. He was surrounded
by the ocean, with the ridge continuing on a mile along
the crest. It wasn't the kind of spot where you'd unpack
and spread your stuff out. Here, you pitched your tent,
shot some pictures, took a deep breath, and then: "You sat

outside the tent on the ledge and watched the sun set below the horizon and talked about the beauty that you are lucky enough to experience."

So it was magic, but also vertiginous. Making matters worse was the fierce wind at night, which battered the tent–an ordeal made ever more harrowing considering the vertical drop below. "To be honest, we didn't get a lot of sleep. The wind was howling up the valley and shaking the tent all night long. The red dirt in the area was pelting against the fabric of the tent, and you could taste the small dust particles that somehow entered through the small openings. I had to keep reminding myself that it's all about the adventure and that day would soon come, but after a few hours you sometimes wonder if you made the right choice." Luckily for them, the wind eventually died down, offering some respite just before dawn.

"After spending a lot of my time in Hawaii in resorts, it was so nice to experience the rawness of the island and its beautiful topography." Jamie's closing words perfectly sum up the perspectives just waiting to open up to those exploring not just Hawaii's secrets but all of nature's hidden gems. With nature, keeping secrets is perennially rewarding–for you, for others, for future generations. Chase your own dream spot and protect it by keeping it secret.

Thanks, Jamie, for not sharing yours.

Oahu Island, Hawaii
Contributed by Jamie Out

HOW TO FIND
A SECRET SPOT

Campers don't always give away their secrets, but here are some ways to find your own hidden campsites. We'll leave the rest up to you.

- Look at a topographic map or Google maps to see what the land is like where you want to camp. Note any trails that might lead to the spot that catches your eye.

- If you're new to camping, don't stray too far off the beaten path—you could get lost or hurt or find that you're tresspassing on someone else's land.

- Keep your ears open and talk to people. Secret campsites are still word of mouth, so chat up the guy at your local REI or share a beer with some hikers on a favorite trail. See if they'll divulge their spots.

- Check out the spot before you commit. You want to be prepared before you think about spending the night somewhere.

Fall colors in Denali National Park, Alaska
Contributed by Simon Prochaska

Troll Lake in Kärkevagge Valley, Sweden
Contributed by Lisa Löwenborg

CAMPING CHRONICLES

Lisa Löwenborg

THE ENCHANTED NIGHT

Trollsjön, or Troll Lake, is the clearest and purest lake in Sweden, composed of meltwater from the surrounding glaciers. It's located at the head of the Kärkevagge Valley, in the most northern part of Sweden.

Most people travel there for the lake, but it's for the actual hike that I always go back. The valley itself is surrounded by fells, but the trail takes you through big, almost surreal boulders. Every time I've camped there, the morning mists have swept around the boulders throughout the valley, and I always make sure to have a cup of coffee in my hand just before the sun hits the mountain ridge to watch the beautiful spectacle in peace. If you're getting up a little too late, head straight for the lake, as it's normally lying still in the mornings, and you'll be able to see all the way to the bottom.

The hike to Trollsjön is not far at all. It's an easy walk uphill from the road. It's getting to the actual start that is trickier. Kärkevagge Valley is over 800 miles away from Stockholm, so if, like me, you're traveling from there, it's a long drive. But reaching Kiruna, driving to the valley past the lake Torneträsk, it's well worth it.

The valley is beautiful in both winter and summer. This photo was taken in early August, when mosquitos are few and the temperature mild. As with pretty much all hiking in northern Sweden, you can drink the water straight from the many streams around. And thanks to Sweden's "freedom to roam" principle, people have the right to freely explore in nature, which means you can put up your tent almost anywhere you want to. And Trollsjön is a place you'd really want to peg your tent.

AURORA CAMP

To spend the night or just take a break and enjoy the peace and quiet, Sakari Hyytinen, founder of 66 Arctic Adventures, set up this traditional *lavvu* hut ten miles from Rovaniemi in Finland. Pointing toward the stars and the aurora borealis, it provides hikers with a quiet refuge and is worth a trip in its own right. In March 2017, Sakari and his photographer friend Miika took advantage of a radiantly clear sky to watch the northern lights. This lively oasis in the middle of the Arctic tundra makes camping an easy trip from the city for anyone who dreams of one day experiencing this celestial ballet.

Traditional Lavvu hut in the Finnish Lapland

Contributed by Miika Hämäläinen

Peter's Stone, in Derbyshire Dales National
Nature Reserve, England

Contributed by Maximilien Czech

PITCH YOUR TENT
ON A PERCH

Peter's Stone, in Derbyshire Dales National Nature Reserve just southeast of Manchester, is one of the most exposed rocks in England. The wind will do its best to tussle with your tent and maybe even try to unhook it. But to sleep outside is to soak up all of nature, and here that includes sound: the whistling of the wind and the buzzing of your tent will enter your dreams.

Peter's Stone is a large block of circular limestone that emerges from the Derbyshire valley, sporting a dense green lawn that promises impeccable floor comfort. Bouldering buffs will surely appreciate the spot. In short, it's a conquering camp experience. If you want a memorable night's sleep, you'll get that here. Not to spoil it, but the view from up top is endless, with no blind spots.

WINDOW ON THE WILD

Whether you're a leisurely hiker or an ambitious climber, what all campers dream about in anticipation of a trip is that moment when you can finally enjoy your assembled tent—with all the comforts of home (or as many as possible) carefully laid out and ready for use. This ideal may be perfectly captured by the American novelist Wallace Stegner in *Where the Bluebird Sings to the Lemonade Springs*: "This place has everything—every essential, every conceivable extra. It has the level ground, the good grass, the wood, the easy access to water, that make a camp comfortable. It has the shelter and shade, the wide views, the openness and breeziness, that raise comfort to luxuriousness."

Then, every morning, as you gradually unzip your fabric door, you'll rediscover the Eden you came to visit—right where you left it the night before—and its unaltered magic. This tent, a magnificent darkroom in the middle of a photographer's paradise, reveals the snapshot as soon as the door opens.

CLOCKWISE FROM TOP LEFT
Coastal view, northern Iceland
Contributed by Timothy Latte

Secret spot, somewhere in the
Italo-Swiss Alps
Contributed by Philipp Heigel

Sunset in Second Beach, Olympic
National Park, Washington State
Contributed by Caroline Walasavage

Rare good-weather moment in
Lofoten Island, Norway
Contributed by Julius Ulbrich

Turnagain Arm banks, Hope, Alaska.
Contributed by Mason Strehl

THE
EXPEDITION

WHILE CAMPING IS ABOUT THE ART OF LIVING, for many,
it's also about the art of staying alive. Many paths would have gone
untrodden, many rocks unclimbed, many vast territories unexplored
were it not for those who dared to take the unbeaten trail. Advanced
techniques and gear have allowed many adventurers and athletes to test
their bodies and their courage in infinitely extreme expeditions.

Imagine: sleeping in -5°F, with violent winds whipping around you, while
you're suspended from a rock cliff 20,000 feet above sea level. Even if
the excitement of being outdoors is the common denominator for every
extreme camper, sleeping and resting become the main goal. Safety and
protection always need to be there, ingrained in the foundations of the
camp. The notion of comfort becomes relative, signaling more a set of
means that make it possible to make it safely to the next day.

These extreme campers don't choose a campsite because it's dreamworthy or comfortable. The spectacle is not always an available option. In many cases you don't get to choose your spot; your pace and the conditions determine it. That's when you need the right gear and the right preparation–because your life depends on it.

In this chapter, meet innovators who have had the will to put their lives, bodies, and gear to the test. They never stop exploring fabrics and technology that will allow them to venture into just about any type of climate or uncharted territory. And you'll learn about their different styles of camp–from the lonely tent-bound on mountainsides, to vertical cliff-hangers, to high-altitude base campers. All of them have precious tips and experiences to share and thrilling photographs that take you to the most thrilling places on earth.

PREVIOUS **Everest Base Camp**
Contributed by Gustav Thuesen

Sunset at Camp 1, Aconcagua, Argentina
Contributed by Grace McDonald

RULES FOR MOUNTAINEERING

When Austin Siadak quit his job in 2011, it was because he wanted to merge his passion for adventure more seamlessly into his life. So he hit the road. Today, having climbed many mountains and edited multiple adventure films, Austin now identifies as a storyteller and climber who lives for authentic experiences, especially those involving mountaineering. "Much of the camping I do happens while I am alpine climbing and mountaineering," Austin says.

First, and this is no trivial matter, every outing of his begins with the backpack. Austin brings only the essentials and keeps weight to a minimum. The camping gear in his backpack includes nothing more than his sleeping kit (no tent) and a small isobutane stove. This cooktop allows him to heat up water for his dinner, make coffee in the morning, and melt snow for drinking water when he's in the alpines.

Southern Patagonian ice cap, between Argentina and Chile
Contributed by Austin Siadak

After a day of climbing or hiking, there comes the time to find an ideal camp spot. For Austin, there are four important qualities that define a camp spot. It has to be flat, close to a source of water, and sheltered, but these three criteria are meaningless without the fourth: it must have a scenic view. Even though, sometimes, you have to take what you can get.

Finding a flat spot for your tent is nonnegotiable. It offers a space to really lie down, stretch out, and relax–something necessary for recharging the body before the next day of effort. In this recovery process, being able to rehydrate is equally important.

That's it for the necessities–although necessity is not the sole motiving factor for how or why Austin camps. Pleasure is just as important. Austin explains, "Looking out over vast mountain landscapes alight with the brilliant hues of sunrise fills me with a childlike sense of awe and wonder, and so I always try to find or position my campsites so that I have a good view of my surroundings."

Whether sleeping in a scenic 360-degree vista is your purpose or just a reward of your escape, the sky is part and parcel of the landscape, and sometimes it forces us to give it up. Weather has the final word when you're choosing a spot, since ultimately staying warm and dry is crucial to your happiness–even if it means forsaking other comforts.

North Cascades National Park,
Washington State

Contributed by Austin Siadak

THE PERFECT TENT

To find the right tent, consider four basic criteria: the mobility of the trip you are planning, the expected weather conditions, the capacity of everything the tent will contain (people and packs), and the type of setup you need.

Consider How Mobile the Tent Needs to Be

Are you heading out on a backpacking trip? Or do you just want to get some fresh air with some weekend car camping? In the former case, since you'll be changing location every day, you'll want a lighter, more compact tent that won't weigh you down or exhaust you when it's time to set up camp after a strenuous day of hiking. To gauge the efficiency of your tent, it's generally assumed that an effective weight for a tent should be around two pounds per person. In other words, if you are two hikers, your tent should not weigh more than four pounds. In the latter case, if you're staying put, there's no need to fuss much over the details—or to skimp on space or comfort. Might as well go big or go home.

Check the Weather and Climate

Depending on the type of activity you're planning and your destination, you might unexpectedly be exposed to fierce winds, baking heat or freezing cold, torrential rains or stifling humidity. There are tents adapted to each of these conditions—that can help shield you from the wind, regulate the temperature, ventilate the humidity, or shelter you from the pounding rain.

Know What Capacity You Require

Tents are made up of different compartments, called the room (where you sleep) and the vestibule (where you leave your stuff). The size and number of each will also depend on what you're doing and the number of comrades you're housing. But the bigger a tent is, the heavier it tends to be. Keep in mind that when backpacking with a group, sometimes it makes more sense to take a couple of smaller tents and divvy up the weight in different packs rather than opting for a three- or four-person tent that'll weigh down the shoulders of the poor person chosen to carry it.

Understand Your Setup Needs

Tent assembly should not be taken lightly. When backpacking, you'll want to be able to quickly assemble your shelter, especially if rain or darkness is impending. You'll also want to pick a tent that is flexible for all types of terrain. So for backpacking, a freestanding pole tent will be a major help, especially in rocky terrain. Get to know your tent before your trip. The more you practice setting it up, the more efficient you'll become.

When car camping, the choice of tent is up to you; there's no shortage of options when you're looking to spend a night outside in optimal conditions. But still make sure to consider the weather and the season for your outing. If you camp every season, opt for a four-season tent to carry you from spring through winter.

TENT GLOSSARY

THE TEPEE OR LAVVU

The traditional tent that inspired modern tents.

THE INFLATABLE GEODESIC TENT

The geodesic structure offers extreme stability. Ideal for adventurers sleeping in windy spots.

THE DOME

The classic hikers' tent.

THE RIDGE TENT

The traditional scouting tent that features plenty of space and comfort. It's the best recreational tent you'll find.

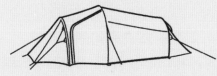

THE TUNNEL

The ultra-light solution for thru-hikers.

THE HIGH-ALTITUDE LIFE

Mountaineering is a world apart from sea-level exploration, with different needs because of the increased altitude. In fact, you can't always just climb a mountain; depending on how high you're aiming, you might need to hike up and back down to acclimate your body to the high-altitude environment. And so, along the way, you'll find whole communities organized to help these efforts—mini economies that prepare and supply backpackers for the ascent ahead. Base camps, the places from which mountaineering expeditions set out, can be organized like little cities, complete with a kitchen and dining tents, postal service, telecommunication area, health area, and more. They are located in crossing paths where most expeditions converge before beginning the route. You'll also find supply hubs, which are kind of tent villages where you can purchase mountain gear and food.

But the higher you go, the less well stocked you'll find these base camps and hubs, so you eventually have to depend on your own self-sufficiency, tent-bound with only the food and sleeping gear you have on your back.

Nesakwatch Spires in the North Cascades,
British Columbia, Canada
Contributed by Grace McDonald

At Ama Dablam base camp with a southwestern view of some of the peaks of the Hinku Himal, Khumbu region, Nepal

Camp 2; a tiny perch of rock on Ama Dablam

Contributed by Grace McDonald

HIMALAYAN CAMP LIFE

with Grace McDonald

GRACE MCDONALD has climbed nine of the fourteen highest mountains on earth and has reached five summits. She has spent many nights in high-altitude base camps. Here, she gives insight into the experience with many invaluable tips.

When starting a new expedition, what is the first camp experience?

Depending on where you're heading, your first night of camping might be your first night of a week-long approach toward the mountain. Every afternoon after four to eight hours of hiking, you arrive at your resting place, pitch tents, and settle in, only to undo it all and repeat day after day until you reach the mountain. The good news is that you're pitching tents because you're in the middle of nowhere, most likely surrounded by stunning scenery and incredible peaks. In the Khumbu region of Nepal (which leads to Everest) you likely will stay in lodges and never see a tent until you arrive at base camp. The same goes for the other side of Everest in Tibet, where you drive right up to your already pitched tent.

How do you feel when you arrive at base camp the first day of an expedition?

Climbing an 8,000-meter (26,000-foot) mountain leads you to base camps that are usually stationed at an altitude anywhere between 4,500 meters and 5,500 meters depending on the mountain; you feel an incredible mix of emotions. On the one hand you have completed a journey; on the other, a journey is just beginning.

Arrival at a base camp is your "in between" moment. It's a brief day of arrival where all the stress of planning and packing and getting to this point falls away, and the new stress of climbing the mountain that looms above you has yet to set in. I try to stay present and soak up the day with ease. I shake off the lingering tiredness of daily packing and unpacking by pulling all my duffel bags to my tent and systematically unpacking them.

In my mind, I'm making my "home" for the next six weeks, and it will be my haven as I work my way up and down the mountain, returning for days of rest and relaxation in between. There's a place for everything: one side pocket holds toiletries and medicine, another for electronics, the next for my writing and reading materials, and on the shelf above my head, a picture of those who remain at home and cannot be with me—as well as a headlamp for easy access.

Tell us more about how base camp cities are organized.

The base camp on the south side of Everest in Nepal is the largest. In some years it's at least a thirty-minute walk from one end to the other. It is a city with many districts. Each district is a team, and each team is serviced by at least one kitchen tent, one dining tent, climber tents, staff tents, bathroom tents, shower tents, and sometimes even communication domes and chill-out domes. There isn't a grocery store, but daily deliveries come via human porters, yaks, and even helicopters. There's an ER hospital tent, and in 2016 there was even an art exhibit tent. It's base camp on steroids.

Usually base camps are much less impressive. Teams still form their own districts and are serviced with a more basic arrangement of a dining tent, kitchen tent, storage tent, and member/staff tents. There are no helicopters, no hospital, and no daily deliveries. If you're lucky, a porter might walk in a yak or goat for slaughter along with a few mangos. If not, then it's rice and potatoes as usual. Organization happens on a team-by-team basis with little coordination at a higher, centralized level. However, there can be much more interaction between teams in such scenarios, as the lack of any centralized governance opens the camp up to more impromptu meetings, dinner invitations, and sometimes even the odd small party.

How is the general mood in a base camp? What do people talk about?

Almost everyone starts out as strangers and ends up with new deep friendships or new sworn enemies. We talk about our families, climbing, personal history, what food we miss, what movie we wished we had on our computer. We get tired. We get grumpy. We get silly. And outside of the walls of our personal base camp tent, we are never alone. That immense shared experience is like no other.

We are stripped of all of our usual retreats and comfort mechanisms and are left with little choice but to be ourselves. There's a beauty in that, and it more often than not leads to incredible, long-term friendships and unforgettable shared moments.

Describe the feeling when you leave base camp for the expedition.

Expeditions on 8,000-meter peaks are usually conducted in a "siege" style. This means that base camp always remains, and we work our way up and down the mountain, gaining altitude and establishing another camp then retreating to base camp after a day or two to rest and let the acclimatization to higher altitude take effect. Often, this is repeated over the course of setting three high camps above base camp, and it takes weeks to amass the necessary number of good weather days to accomplish this. Ultimately, we always return to base camp for a final rest before a full attempt up, up, up, and up to the summit.

It can be hard leaving base camp, as you go from days of relatively little activity to full on physical pushes to a higher altitude in unknown terrain. It's a mental game to psych yourself up for the complete switch in activity level. At the same time, there is a sense of excitement at finally getting to move. Most people struggle with the down time in base camp more than the up time on the mountains.

Generally, up to around 6,500 meters, I quite enjoy the nights of being tent-bound on a mountainside. It's a good day of physical effort in incredible surroundings followed by an afternoon and evening of better views than the best hotel in the world. It can also be incredibly comforting and even empowering to know that you are surrounded by everything that you need—basic though it may be. You have a sleeping pad, a sleeping bag, food, a stove, and even a tent mate or maybe two. It's definitely cozy.

Above 6,500 meters the physical aspects of altitude can become quite bothersome—particularly headaches and general malaise—and that's when you're feeling pretty good. It's a grin-and-bear-it grind, but it often comes at the very end of your final acclimatization round on the mountain and will only be repeated on your summit push. It's temporary. On the plus side, the views get better and better, but so do your summit dreams and worries.

In such extreme conditions, what is the protocol for when the time has come to set up camp?
In challenging conditions, it's important that everyone stays on their game, does not rest, and moves as quickly and efficiently as possible to establish a platform and tent for retreat. Once inside, everyone can take a moment to plan further actions depending on weather. There is such a thing as too many cooks in the kitchen when setting up a tent. In that case, let there be one chef and follow his lead.

Is there a pleasure somewhere in camping in these conditions?
When you live with so many comforts on a daily basis, living without is often the best way to take immense pleasure in all that you so often live with. You find yourself back in base camp experiencing joy as you slip on a fresh pair of underwear, sit in a chair, eat a fried egg.

On top of that, camping in these conditions can provide the perfect opportunities for special moments of kindness and compassion. Your tent mate might wake up first to light the stove, share their iPod playlist with you, or offer you a bite of their chocolate—the last one they carried all the way up. It can bring out the best in us.

How important are the porters?
Porters are vital to the task of even getting to the mountain with all of your food and gear. They operate under a single lead porter carrying heavy loads and moving quickly day after day to get you to your next destination. They are often young men from nearby villages, and this job is their only method of getting actual cash in hand to supplement the lives they lead primarily by living off the land. Without them, remote expeditions would not happen as regularly as they happen now.

What would you say to people who dream of sleeping on a mountain?
Nothing on this earth lights up our imagination the way nature does. It's no wonder we love spending our nights surrounded by its splendor. No one should live a life without a night like this. The higher you get the more you see, but take your time, as nature also demands respect, and there is a lot to learn.

Start locally by heading to your highest hill and camping out for a night. Next, expand your boundaries and head to a more remote place where you can hike to an elevated area and camp out for the night, below the snow line. In the winter, go camp outside for a night. Maybe head to a local glaciated area and take a one-day glacier skills course, so you can start understanding the nature of that environment. Next, look around for a high-altitude training course. Not only will you learn some basic mountaineering skills, but you'll also get to spend your first night high up on a snowy peak taking in a widescreen view of all that nature can offer.

NEXT PAGE Grace's expedition team moving from Camp 1 to Camp 2, on Shishapangma, Tibet Autonomous region, China
contributed by Grace McDonald

"When you live with so many comforts on a daily basis, living without is often the best way to take immense pleasure in all that you so often live with."

CAMPING
CHRONICLES

James Barkman

MOUNTAINEERING IN
BRITISH COLUMBIA

We had scrambled up 2,000 vertical feet of fourth- or fifth-class loose scree and rockfall on Mount Robson in British Columbia. The straps from our seventy-pound packs rubbed into our shoulders, and the thousands of feet of exposure forced us to focus intently on every move. We were following an obscure climbers' route known as the Patterson Spur. Toward evening, we topped out on the ridgeline and traversed over rocky towers in freezing temperatures.

Eventually, we found a flat snowy area along the ridgeline that was large enough to pitch our tent. We used our ice axes and screws to stake the tent into the ice. At 10,000 feet, the wind was stronger and the air colder. I peeked my head out of the tent and noticed the sky turning into a greenish hue. It wasn't long before the hue grew stronger, and for a couple hours the Northern Lights lit up and danced across the moonless sky. I crawled back into our tent, safe from the wind and cold for a few short hours, thinking of what challenges we would face the next day on our climb.

Mount Robson, via the Patterson Spur,
Canadian Rocky Mountains,
British Columbia
Contributed by James Barkman

THE ALPINE GRADING SYSTEM

Every country has developed its own classification for alpine climbs. The U.S. National Climbing Classification System (NCCS) includes seven grades, called "commitment grades," which refer to the difficulty of each climbing route. They offer information about the time it takes an "average" climbing team to complete the route.

I & II: A maximum of a half-day of rope climbing

III: Almost a full day of rope climbing

IV: A full day of technical rope climbing

V: A full day plus an overnight on the route (or can be done in a day in a fast and free way)

VI: A minimum of two hard climbing days

VII: Remote walls climbed in alpine style

Ascent of the East Buttress of Mount Whitney, California, the highest point in the continental United States

Contributed by James Barkman

HORIZONTAL HAVEN

It's springtime, the dry season, when Alexis Jarry heads into Sagarmatha National Park–home to Mount Everest. Destination: Renjo La Pass. Elevation: 17,500 feet. He's heard about a little open ledge used by Sherpas, offering one of the most complete views of Mount Everest–and a camping oasis in the middle of this vertical territory.

The final ascent begins at the village of Gokyo. It'll require four hours of hiking. Amid stones and scree, Alexis keeps his balance and moves along steadily, his body in tune with his feet. Despite this terrain, his heavy pack, and recent events that could have pinned Alexis to the mountain floor–the valley–he keeps his head up and keeps moving forward. Such recent events include the deadliest avalanche in Mount Everest's history, which took the lives of sixteen Nepalese guides and shook up the whole community of Solukhumbu District. That happened two days before Alexis's departure for Renjo La. Emotional and respectful, Alexis sticks to his plan.

After eighteen days on-site, Alexis is prepared and adjusted to the altitude. His acclimatization process included hiking six days through mid-range mountains from the village of Shivalaya south of Solukhumbu in order to reach the Everest national park. Then, he gradually increased his altitude in the park using villages as bases for more strenuous treks with lightened backpacks, before spending an overnight trip at the base camp of Cho Oyu (18,700 feet). He repeated daily treks from the villages during twelve days before feeling ready for his own Everest.

Renjo-La Pass, Sagarmatha National Park, Nepal

Contributed by Alexis Jarry

Panorama view of Mount Everest from Renjo-La

Contributed by Alexis Jarry

And yet Alexis still has one more challenge to meet. Despite his efforts to keep his pack light, he's still trudging along with fifty-five pounds on his back–his main hardship, he says. He did everything he could to optimize with a Husky self-supporting tent, a Deuter sleeping bag, a Therm-a-Rest sleeping pad, and a camp stove. His photo equipment, thirteen pounds to capture his expedition as an eternal experience, makes up the rest of the load that's weighing on Alexis's shoulders. But what would be the point of trekking all the way up there–to the finest vantage point in all the Himalayas–without it? "The lead-up to the opening of the pass was ideal for viewing a good portion of the national park, with the enormous Ngozumpa glacier down below in the Gokyo Valley and its sacred lakes and endless majestic peaks on the horizon, including Mount Everest."

So if fifty-five pounds is what it takes, then so be it. Renjo-La Pass is along a monthlong hike on which Alexis mostly camped. On those nights he didn't sleep outdoors, he sought refuge in traditional Nepalese lodges run by welcoming families. It's worth noting that around Mount Everest, the Roof of the World isn't home to a ton of camping spots. Most of the time, the mountain's verticality forces you to head back down to gentler slopes. But at Renjo-La, the Sherpas have leveled off the land to create a rudimentary but necessary place to find rest. This is Alexis's heaven. Those fifty-five pounds be damned.

THE ULTIMATE SHELTER

In September 2010, Walter Krummenacher, the cofounder
of the camping brand Polarmond, had a vision and plan
for keeping people alive. Before even thinking about
adventurers, he wanted to develop the world's best outdoor
sleeping system for homeless people and refugees. His goal
was to protect them from the cold and, in the worst-case
scenario, death.

Inventing the ultimate sleeping system meant
sorting through and prioritizing the countless variables
possible. First, Walter had to define what he saw as its
most important overall functions. The shelter would have
to be self-warming (no use of external energy), provide
a complete fresh air supply, offer air-suspended comfort,
avoid heat accumulation, and be lightweight. From this list
emerged Polarmond's All-In-One Sleep System.

Krummenacher and his partner, Marcel Schubiger,
developed several prototypes, which they first tested in
the climate cold chamber at Empa, the Swiss Federal
Laboratories for Materials Science and Technology. Initial
results were satisfactory, since the cold chamber tested the
tent at -20°F, but the tent was too heavy to be considered a
complete success. After tweaking the design and bringing
the weight down, they field-tested their sleeping system at

the top of Europe, at the Jungfraujoch Firn in Switzerland. Up there, the revamped prototype of their tent experienced truly extreme conditions. The temperature reached as low as -20°F accompanied by heavy snowstorms–perfect conditions, in other words, to usher their innovation into the real outdoor world.

Today, their All-In-One Sleep System can sustain most weather conditions: snow, heavy rain, high winds up to 60 miles per hour. The sleeping chamber keeps the temperature well regulated inside, even when outside temperatures range from -20°F to 75°F. With their system, Walter and Marcel raised the standards for extreme expeditions, allowing adventurers to sleep in warm and dry comfort. And for claustrophobic folks who don't enjoy the confined space of sleeping bags, a major plus of their creation is that you won't even need one.

Since camping is also about living in harmony with wildlife, Polarmond includes in its technical specifications a complete commitment to animal welfare: "We really don't support plucking down from live geese. Polarmond defined a high-tech artificial fiber as insulation material."

So this really is the ultimate shelter: not only does it protect adventurers and animals, but it also opens the door for explorers to venture farther into the most extreme places. You're only limited by your imagination.

BIVOUAC BOREALIS

Setting up a polar tent site is a matter of timing, where cold is the minute hand and darkness the second hand. As they both impose their own rhythm, you have to be extremely vigilant and fast. The campsite has to be chosen during day hours, because once the night starts to appear, temperatures decrease drastically.

It's the middle of winter in February 2017 when Charles Lopez and a friend land in Finnish Lapland not far from Inari, about two hundred miles above the Arctic Circle. For one week, they'll get to experience the glacial cold.

To ease his way in and help him adapt from the comfort of home to the harshness of a polar bivouac, Charles spends a few days in a cabin without running water or electricity, where he'll photograph Tinja and Alex, two breeders in the Muotkatunturi Wilderness Area who share their farm with eighty-five sled dogs, five Siberian and Icelandic horses, and an indeterminate number of free-roaming reindeer. In a couple of days, he'll set off with Tinja and Alex on a polar camping expedition.

At fifteen degrees below zero, Charles is learning that two things are absolutely critical: keeping the stove going, the only source of heat and the only way to have a hot meal, and fetching water from the river. The river water is actually flowing, but under a thick slab of ice, and it's two hundred yards away. That takes some work. Armed with an ice pick and ice saw, he spends half an hour boring through twenty inches of ice to extract the river water. To drink, cook, or bathe, he'll have to repeat the effort. In this cold, the ice closes up again quickly.

Bivouac beyond the Arctic Circle, Finnish Lapland

Contributed by Charles Lopez

Dog sledding in the Muotkatunturi
Wilderness Area, Finnish Lapland
Contributed by Charles Lopez

"Halfway through my stay, after I familiarized myself with the sled dogs, we headed out for two days of camping in the Muotkatunturi Wilderness Area. There were six of us. After twenty-five miles, we found a perfect spot to set up camp atop a hill. We'd been on the sleds for hours; all you could see was endless white. Tinja and Alex were looking for a clearing that was slightly elevated yet with some trees to lash the dogs to." And what makes a perfect spot in this landscape and in such harsh conditions? Charles doesn't hesitate: "Every place in the entire natural reserve is a perfect spot!"

It's time for the choreography to begin. Everyone has to be precise, organized, and in sync with the rest of the team. The night and the cold loom large. The days are extremely short: it'll be too dark to work by 4 p.m., so the group has just two hours to get everything set up. They have to start by installing the straw dog beds and feeding the team of dogs–ninety pounds of meat to distribute to over three dozen dogs.

Meanwhile, the camp is being assembled from only top-notch materials. The team will slumber in army tents, at once super light and sturdy. On the ground, reindeer-skin sleeping pads will insulate these foolhardy folk from the cold. To round it all off, Charles has brought his big down sleeping bag, ideal at five degrees below zero, but which hardly wavers at the fifteen below shown on the thermometer.

Around 5:30 p.m., the camp is finally set up. Night has long fallen. In total darkness, lit up only by the campfire and their headlights, the team enjoys the spectacle in the sky. Huge green undulations make the scene extra special. Charles is experiencing his first aurora borealis. The moment is as fleeting as it is entrancing: in this cold and darkness, you don't linger long outside.

Charles and the others will hit the sack rather early. Once alone, "there's not much left to do other than bundle up as best you can and sip a good old Cuban rum to stay warm." While waiting for sleep to come, Charles becomes more cognizant of the outside noises; he hears the dogs barking but isn't worried. Lying between the free flow of the aurora borealis and the stiffness of the cold, he awaits sleep in utter peace and quiet. He knows the bears are hibernating now, and the sounds raising the dogs' hackles are probably just those of a rash, stubborn reindeer–maybe the same one that had been ahead of them scouting the entire way.

"In the morning, it's something else. You wake up with your stuff completely frozen, including your sleeping bag. First you have to work up the courage to drag yourself out of the sleeping bag and get dressed. Once you're out of the tent, you discover an absolutely majestic scene, with the cold and the rising sun creating a sort of beam jutting straight out of the sky. It's truly a rare and magical moment."

Setting up a polar camp under an aurora borealis
Contributed by Charles Lopez

"Once you're all bundled up, you start to forget the biting cold, and the camp life around the fire is really nice."

VERTICAL CAMP

Stéphanie Bodet and Arnaud Petit are a duo, partners in
climbing and life. Together, they charted new routes on
many big walls and pushed past their limits along the cliffs.
Their numerous vertical adventures have led them to spend
nights on the rock face, though their first time was unplanned.
It was in Tsraranoro, at 6,500 feet up the Central Highlands
in Madagascar.

They wasted too much time in the beginning–their pace
was not fast enough. At the end of the day, it was too dangerous
to rappel down in the dark, so they made the effort to climb
the last 250 feet and improvise a tent on the summit. Despite
the discomfort, cold, and hunger, they discovered very quickly
that, weirdly, they liked it. This step outside their comfort zone
pushed them to plan–really, strategize–to bivvy more often
on the wall. Since then, they may have spent more nights on
the wall than in a bedroom . . . the magic gets the upper hand.

Vertical camp can be synonymous with more freedom,
more time, more height–it opens possibilities. It changes your
perception and the sensations of climbing. Sleeping on the rock
face involves much more gear that you have to haul up the wall.
It makes the ascent more complex, and you lose the sense of
lightness typical of a one-day climb. As compensation, you ease
into a kind of necessary slowness, and this totally changes
your relationship with time.

Stéphanie explains that "hours expand, and you're fully present in what you're doing." According to this voracious climber, there is something very satisfying about carrying your shelter and having to set it up, in one way or another. When the night falls, you're just like prehistoric humankind: at the mercy of nature. On the wall, there is an absolute necessity to be able to set up your home. This requires a bit of planning and practice on artificial climbing walls with experts, as assembling a portaledge, a bed suspended in midair, is not innate. Climbing is the first skill you need to master, but cliff-hanger sleeping is another ball game.

In many camping adventures, you choose your path, then your camp spots. Quite different with climbing depending on whether you're trad or sport climbing. In the first, you open a new route so you will find your spot on the way. In the second, you know the route before you start the climb, so you can determine where you'll set the camp. When you set a route up a cliff, you don't know the pace you'll be keeping, since it depends on the difficulty of the wall. It's fairly slow-going, since you need to set the anchors as you go–a highly technical skill. You generally rarely get more than 300 feet the first day. At that point, it's easiest to just climb back down the wall to camp. That way, you can avoid hauling too much gear. The bivouac becomes necessary after the second climbing day, when you're too high to consider returning to the ground floor.

"I like when the most forbidding of walls offers natural nests for us birds of passage."

Vertical camp on Angel Falls
Photograph by Nicolas Kalisz, contributed by Arnaud Petit

THE LINE OF SIGHT

Before setting a route, Stéphanie explains that they take
some time to study the wall through binoculars to try
to imagine the "line"–that is, the path they're going to
take. Stéphanie remembers an ascent in Morocco when
"we were getting stoked about sleeping on a ledge that
we'd staked out through the binoculars from the ground,
and which was located 2,000 feet up, at the foot of a nice
limestone turret slightly jutting off the wall."

Even if the line determines the ascent first, climbers
usually have an ideal type of spot where they like to
suspend their camp. Stéphanie has a preference for vertical
or sloping sections rather than overhangs, which make the
portaledge less stable and not particularly pleasant. But
having some sort of a ledge is always a plus for Stéphanie,
even if it's just half a foot wide. This lets her set down the
camp stove away from the portaledge and make some extra
space. It is not only a question of comfort but also of safety,
as sleeping bags are very flammable. You want to rule out
any risk of setting your camp ablaze.

A portaledge is barely 20 square feet, if that. Stéphanie
and Arnaud sleep head to toe to make more room.

SUSPEND THE NIGHT

The upside of a portaledge is that it can be set up anywhere, day or night, and only takes ten minutes to construct. Once it is done, what does an evening suspended look like? Many of us may never know, so we'll have to take Stéphanie's word for it: "There's the creaking of the metal tubes against the rock when you move and the noise of the wind whistling through the straps to remind you that you're not at home. Not to mention finding yourself attached to the harness (which you always keep on during the climb) when you wake up!"

Contrary to what I could imagine, Stéphanie assures me that there's no fear of getting woken up during the night. As weird as it sounds, you have a nice sense of security up there. You won't hear a growl or a suspicious sound in the underbrush, contrary to forest camp nights. The only thing you care about is the weather, because even if you did the job well and took into account conditions, luck can wear off.

In Angel Falls, Venezuela, Stéphanie and Arnaud suffered a very uncomfortable night. A big storm with pouring rain intensified a nearby waterfall. They remember being constantly pelted by gusts of spray—an insane scenario at a thousand feet above the ground! Otherwise, the days are so strenuous and your energy spent that she reassures me you sleep really well. Once camp is set, you can look forward to succumbing to rest and relief.

Stéphanie Bodet getting some rest on Angel Falls
Contributed by Arnaud Petit

"I love waking halfway up a vertical cliff, with huge exposure below, no easy way back down to the ground, and lots of challenging climbing above."

El Capitan ascent, Yosemite National Park
Contributed by Alexandre Eggermont

NEXT PAGE
Squamish, British Columbia
Contributed by Alexandre Eggermont

P. 231
Lijiang, Yunnan, China
Contributed by Alexandre Eggermont

THE MODERN PORTALEDGE

with John Deucey Middendorf

With an engineering background, a passion for fabric architecture, and deep experience in climbing, **JOHN DEUCEY MIDDENDORF** (also known as JDM) is a guru of the portaledge, the hanging tent that is meant to suspend from the side of a cliff. In 1986, a violent storm showed John how dangerous portaledges could be, which prompted him to innovate the ultimate fail-safe sleep system that can sustain just about any kind of weather or conditions: the A5 Portaledge. John tells us more about how he evolved the vertical tent.

Is the portaledge a natural playground for you?
I love waking halfway up a vertical cliff, with huge exposure below, no easy way back down to the ground, and lots of challenging climbing above. There is something about the feeling of being committed to a climb that brings out the best in a person. When I started climbing and first saw the walls of Yosemite, I knew the ultimate experience for me would be to climb the tallest cliffs, which require spending multiple days and nights on the wall. The portaledge is simply the tool that allows full rest, protection from the elements, and a nice perch to appreciate the surroundings.

Describe how the portaledge works.
A portaledge is a deployable hanging tent, with a metal frame and fabric bed, that hangs from a single point. The single point is essential for climbing because there often are not anchors

available that are spread out for a two-point hammock, for example. Sleeping in a portaledge is quite comfortable. If you have ever lain on a trampoline, sleeping on a portaledge is quite similar—you feel very secure and stable.

Would you describe your first night on a portaledge?
A lot of the easier routes in Yosemite, like the Nose on El Capitan and the Robbins route on Half Dome, have natural ledges, so you don't need a portaledge. But after doing those, I wanted to do some harder routes. I hooked up with Alex Lowe in 1984, and we climbed what was then the fastest ascent of the longer routes on the Southeast Face of El Capitan. We climbed the route "Hockalito" (a link-up of Hockey Night in Canada—ours was the third ascent—and Mescalito). We spent three nights in portaledges. We were moving too fast to really appreciate the lovely lounge time that can be had in portaledges, but I was amazed at how well one could sleep using a portaledge and be rested and in top performance for the next full day of challenges.

In 1986, a storm tested you and the portaledge severely on the Half Dome. What happened?
Steve Bosque, Mike Corbett, and I started up the South Face of Half Dome, a route put up by Warren Harding, which had very few repeats [that is, not many climbers had done the route again]. We started in nice weather, but when we were at

the "point of no return" (a place on every big wall where it is easier to go up than down), we got hit by one of the worst storms in Yosemite's recorded history, despite all forecasts predicting nice weather when we started. The portaledges of the day were not up for the severity of the storm. The lightweight ripstop flies shredded in the severe winds, and two out of three of our portaledge frames collapsed due to overloading from the ice and snow that piled up on us during the storm. We nearly died of hypothermia the second night, and would certainly have died were we not rescued by a helicopter in a short lull of the third day of the storm.

When you decided to reinvent the portaledge, what was the priority?
Lightweight, small packed size, easy to deploy, and stormproof. The A5 portaledges were the first to be truly stormproof and really precipitated a huge boom in big wall standards around the world in the late 1980s and 1990s. It was the first time big wall climbers could go up in any conditions and be assured of survival, even in the worst Himalayan storms. The A5 portaledges have stood the test of time, and all the modern designs (Black Diamond, Metolius, and a few others) are clones of the A5 engineered design.

What was your best vertical camp experience?
So many fit this description! For me, it was about the partner. I had incredible times climbing with Walt Shipley, Steve Quinlan, Werner Braun, Derek Hersey, Mugs Stump, and Xaver Bongard to name a few. Probably the time Xaver and I withstood a three-day storm at 19,500 feet on Great Trango Tower was the best. The wind, which on a wall comes straight up, was lifting the entire ledge with

us in it, and crashing down. For that route, I had designed a super lightweight titanium frame, and I kept wondering if I had done all the calculations correctly. But it withstood. Seeing clear sky for the first time in days, knowing we were blessed with a weather window for the summit, was magic.

For those who will never sleep on a wall, could you tell us how magical it is?
Just sleeping outside in a remote place is half of the magic. The other half is the way the wall energizes—sleeping in the middle of a sea of granite, looking forward to seeing the sun peek out from around another part of the wall because there's a full day of fun ahead. Portaledges are really quite comfortable, too. One feels quite cradled during the experience.

Tom Laker, English photographer, has developed a very singular way to use the portaledge. Far from climbing walls, Tom camps suspended from trees. From the highest trees. Here, he slept high up in the cedar forest in the Atlas Mountains, Morocco.
Contributed by Tom Laker

THE WINDPROOF TENT

Stefan Clauss and Stefan Schulze-Dieckhoff were on a surfing trip along the gusty Portugal coast when they first started brainstorming about the "tent of the future." The only thing they knew was that tents on the market didn't really speak to them or match their idea of adventure. The duo of Stefans teamed up with, of all things, the wind to devise their first tent: the Cave, a groundbreaking lightweight design that is entirely inflatable and uses minimal hardware. Then they created their company HeimPlanet to launch their project–and a new generation of tents made for more extreme conditions.

Stefan and Stefan both love living in the city, but in nature they expect to experience, well, nature, even in its rawest forms. In other words, they're game for enduring bad conditions, but not with bad equipment. There is a Norwegian saying that goes, "There's no such thing as bad weather, only bad clothes." That also applies to tents and all types of gear.

When pitching your tent takes so much time, you're bound to get soaked to the bone in inclement weather–exactly what they experienced on their Portugal trip. So rain and wind defined how they wanted to reinvent the tent, and they conceived of one that would be "durable, very easy to handle and designed in a completely new way."

From the very beginning, the main defining factor was stability. Applying the principles of geodesic architecture–the most stable structure yet known to humanity–to their inflatable structure, Stefan and Stefan made their Cave much more stable than traditional tents. Building on this success, they developed a line of lightweight tents more suitable for hiking, too, since the wind blows in the mountains just as it does along the coast, after all.

"Spending a couple
of days outside,
away from your
daily routine, works
like magic."

Trolltunga rock formation, Norway
Contributed by Max Münch

If HeimPlanet has changed the DNA of the tent structure, they also foster a camping vision in their company mission. "Spending a couple of days outside, away from your daily routine, works like magic," they say. So they held a Season Opening Camp, a program that brought employees and partners together to try out new things in the wilderness in a fun and relaxed environment. People gradually settled in and found their niche playing a crucial role for the team: Some tended to the campfire; others preferred cooking or scoping out a camp spot. With camping, there's always a way for everyone to get involved, and it can be a learning experience that benefits both individual and collective.

For the two Stefans, the essence of a great camp experience–no matter where or in what conditions–is simplicity. Camping is about getting back to basics and relishing the day as it unfolds before you. "We all have a strong connection to nature, and it makes us feel good to connect with it. Staying outside for the night only intensifies this experience and is the icing on the cake. It is one of the most luxurious experiences, to wake up in the middle of nature. It lifts you up while keeping you grounded at the same time."

THE HEIGHTS OF SLOVAKIA

Maciek Maciejowski, a Polish photographer and founder of the outdoor clothes brand WildRootWear, likes to call Slovakia the Canada of Central Europe. Almost two-thirds of this small nation is covered by mountains, and you'll find forests everywhere. The population density is low, and the variety of the landscape very rich–in other words, it's a European Canada.

Mount Veľký Choč is a beacon in the north of the country. Admittedly, it is far from being the highest point in Slovakia, with just 5,000 feet of altitude. But it rises in the heart of the Slovakian's peak mountains and offers a breathtaking view of them up to the Carpathians: Mount Pilsko to the north, the High Tatras to the east, the Tatras to the south, and the Malá Fatra to the west. In good weather, you may even get to see them all at the same time. If, by chance, the clouds swoop down into the valley, all these peaks would then separate from each other and form a floating archipelago in the sky. And you would be camping there, on the Veľký Choč "island" amid this cottony sea.

When Maciek hiked this mountain recently, it wasn't particularly hospitable. He had never felt so cold–the temperature was 5°F, and it was snowing. His plan to take photos of the Milky Way quickly vanished, with visibility close to zero. The wind was gusting at fifty miles per hour. Nature did everything it could to complicate setting up camp. As Maciek acknowledges, "We had enormous problems pitching our tent."

But the next day, in the early morning hours, the clouds began to fall into the valley, opening up a surprise panorama. Just like that, they witnessed a total inversion of natural conditions, and a glorious landscape was revealed.

Mount Veľký Choč, Slovakia

Contributed by Maciek Maciejowksi

NEXT PAGE Mer et Monde campground,

Saint Lawrence River, Québec

CAMPING HACKS

With all this discussion of camping, it's worth remembering that no matter how perfectly we plan, we do not own nature and are at its whims. We have to be able to adapt and live with the conditions it imposes. But it's possible to apply some method to the madness; all it takes is some simple but sly tricks. Want to know how to light a match when the wind is blowing at fifty miles per hour? Or how to cook without a stove? Read on.

MATCHSTICK *in the* WIND

A measly flame is no match for a strong gust. When the wind won't stop blowing, bring out your trusty knife.

What you need: a matchstick and a sharp knife

1. Pull out a matchstick.
2. Use your knife to gently cut into the upper portion of the matchstick and fray the stick just beneath the head. You should end up with attached pieces of wood curling up toward the head. Be careful not to weaken the end of the match too much or you won't be able to strike it.
3. When you strike the match, the flame should burn brightly despite the wind.

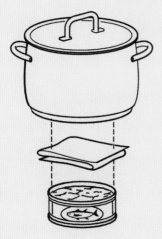

the TUNA CAN STOVE

Use the age-old technology of the candle—oil, wick, and flame—to cook a meal anywhere.

What you'll need: one can oil-packed tuna, toilet paper (bear with me), matches, and a small pot of rice with water

1. Open a tuna can.
2. Place two sheets of toilet paper on top, letting them soak up oil.
3. Light the four corners of the sheets of toilet paper.
4. Place a pot of rice over the flaming can.
5. Let the tuna and rice cook together until the rice is done.
6. Enjoy!

TOOTHPASTE DOTS

Skip the big tube of toothpaste and prepare your dental hygiene a few days before you leave.

What you'll need: toothpaste, wax paper, and a tiny box

1. On a sheet of wax paper, press out the number of dabs of toothpaste you'll need for morning, noon, and night.
2. Let the dabs dry, then place them in the box.
3. On your trip, pop a dab in your mouth to rehydrate it and begin brushing. Smile!

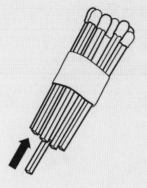

the BIG BLAZE

Start a campfire more easily with a torch that has a big and long-lasting flame.

What you need: adhesive tape, matches

1. Bundle together six matches and tape them together.
2. Gently push down the matchstick in the middle.
3. Forcefully push it up to ignite the bundle.
4. Boom! You should get a big flame.

the GREEN LANTERN

This hack is useful if you have only one headlamp and need a bigger source of light.

What you need: a transparent water bottle, a headlamp

1. Place your headlamp around your water bottle.
2. Face the beam inward to the water bottle.
3. And there was light! The water bottle will disperse the light like a lantern.

the CHEAP FIRE-STARTER KIT

Lighting a campfire should not cost an arm and a leg. Build a starter kit for your next trip.

What you need: charcoal and a cardboard egg carton (for six or twelve eggs, depending on the size of your campfire)

1. Place the egg carton in the firepit; then place a charcoal briquette in each egg holder.
2. Carefully light the egg carton. Once the cardboard burns away, the charcoal should be sufficiently burning.

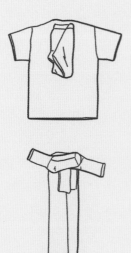

HACK-PACKING

Make sure your spare clothes don't take up more space than a pair of socks.

What you need: nothing more than your change of clothes (a pair of socks, a T-shirt, underpants)

1. Lay your T-shirts flat.
2. Place your underpants along the back of your T-shirts.
3. Fold the right sleeve, then the left sleeve on your underpants.
4. Place flat the foot part of your socks along the neck of your T-shirt, so that the ankle of each sock lines up with the sides of the tee.
5. Roll up each tee, from the neck to the bottom. Now everything is packed inside the T-shirt except the sock ankles.
6. Turn the ankle of the sock around the T-shirt roll.

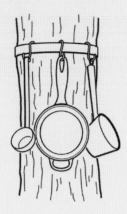

the TREE BELT

Build a pan holder to keep your camp tidy.

What you need: a belt and S-hooks

1. Wrap the belt around a tree trunk.
2. Arrange the S-hooks in the holes around the belt.
3. Clean up your camp by hanging the handles of your pots on the S-hooks.

SAGE REPELLENT

Use this natural repellent when you're concerned about bugs but don't want to turn to chemicals.

What you need: a bundle of dried sage and string

1. Make a generous bouquet of sage and tie the stems tight with string, allowing extra length for hanging.
2. Light the dried bundle.
3. Hang it up or place it near your group. The smoke will deter bugs.

Along the path leading to
Tardevant Peak, French Alps
Contributed by Matthieu Tober

RESOURCES

Here is a list of inspiration I collected while creating *Camp.*

BOOKS

How to Stay Alive in the Woods by Bradford Angier

Indian Creek by Pete Fromm

The Lost Grizzlies by Rick Bass

Microadventures by Alastair Humphreys

Scouting for Boys by Lord Robert Baden-Powell

To Build a Fire by Jack London

MAGAZINES

BESIDE

Ernest Journal

Sidetracked

Waves and Woods

INSTAGRAM

@bornwild

@campingcollective

@camp4collective

@camptrend

@lucgesell

@Ourcamplife

@smokeybear

@survivalist_outdoors

@thetentcommandments

SUPPLY STORES

Au Vieux Campeur
France
auvieuxcampeur.fr

Best Made Company
New York, NY; and Los Angeles, CA
bestmadeco.com

Cabela's
cabelas.com

CAMP
Whistler, BC, Canada

Camp Brand Goods
Calgary, Alberta, Canada
campbrandgoods.com

Iron and Resin
San Francisco, CA
ironandresin.com

La Cordée
Montreal and Quebec City, Quebec, Canada
lacordee.com/en

Poler Stuff
Portland, OR;
Laguna Beach, CA
polerstuff.com

REI
Rei.com

Sanborn Canoe Company
Winona, MN
sanborncanoe.com

Topo Design
San Francisco, CA;
Boulder and Denver, CO
topodesigns.com

United by Blue
Philadelphia, PA;
New York, NY
unitedbyblue.com

CAMPING EXPERIENCES

66 Arctic Adventures
Rovaniemi, Finland
66arcticeadventures.fi

Camp Rockaway
Rockaway Park, NY
camprockaway.com

Hipcamp
hipcamp.com

Mer et Monde Ecotours
Quebec, Canada
meretmonde.ca/en

Satori Adventures and Expeditions
satoriexpeditions.com

Siperia
Inari Wilderness Area of Muotkatunturi, Finland
siperia.eu/

Trekker Adventures
New Zealand
www.trekkeradventures.com

Vildmark i Värmland
Värmland, Sweden
vildmark.se

ACKNOWLEDGMENTS

ABOVE ALL, I WANT TO THANK my fantastic and thoughtful editor, Angelin Borsics, who has given me this opportunity to realize not only a book but a wonderful life project. My first book.

This project would also not exist without every contributor involved in this book–the photographers, innovators, outdoor enthusiasts, surfers, hikers, climbers, riders . . . and campers. You all are this book. A special thanks to the early ones who trusted me when the project was still nothing: Mason Strehl, Benjamin Kinadeter, Roman Königshofer, Charles Lopez, Grace McDonald, Stéphanie Bodet and Arnaud Petit, and John Middendorf. And to Graeme Owsianski, who played an important part in the making of this book.

Camp might have begun with the experiences of many inspiring souls, but other talented and committed people brought it to life: Mia Johnson, who designed the entire book; Kim Tyner, who proofed every image to perfection; Mark Birkey, the one who "left no trace" of any mistakes; and Aislinn Belton, who guided us along the deadlines. I am so grateful for the passion you have all put into *Camp*. Thank you very much to my publishing house, Clarkson Potter, which gathered this team and their means around me to make this book a reality.

Thanks also go to two other valuable members of my team: Nicholas LoVecchio, who translated my words and ideas from French to English. And to Léo, my close friend, I'll never forget that *Camp* took its initial forms at the mythic 255. Your talent and friendship have been precious to me.

All along this journey, I've been lucky enough to meet generous and open-minded people. Anne Cantin-Hofstede from *GEO* magazine, who offered me a few pages to talk about camping and about the book when it was still only in the beginning stages. François Barbe, founder of the sound-production company Men at Work, who helped me create a very professional promotional video and offered precious support. As I'm finishing this book, you both are in my thoughts.

I've opened this book with a few words to my wife, Fanny, and I'll close it the same way. We can spend our life coming up with ideas, but if they stay in our head, they are just wasted projects. Fanny picked this book idea up from my head and told me, "OK, now stop looking for ideas and go with this one." Thank you.

**TO ALL OF YOU, I WISH UNFORGETTABLE MOMENTS
IN THE GREAT OUTDOORS . . .**

INDEX

Note: Page numbers in *italics* indicate photo captions.

Copyright © 2019 by Luc Gesell

All rights reserved.

Published in the United States by
Clarkson Potter/Publishers, an imprint of
the Crown Publishing Group, a division
of Penguin Random House LLC, New York.
crownpublishing.com
clarksonpotter.com

CLARKSON POTTER is a trademark and
POTTER with colophon is a registered
trademark of Penguin Random House LLC.

Library of Congress Cataloging-in-
Publication Data is available upon request.

ISBN 978-0-525-57725-6
Ebook ISBN 978-0-525-57726-3

Printed in China

Cover and interior design by Mia Johnson
Illustrations by Tobatron

10 9 8 7 6 5 4 3 2 1

First Edition